"His lucid prose brings to mind Poe's Gothic horror, Hunter S. Thompson's strangeness (without the drug-craze), and William Burroughs's ellipsis (without the disintegration)."

—*The Globe and Mail*

"The pulse of his words . . . produces a trance-like state in the reader. . . . The words blend and sing."

—*The Globe and Mail*

". . . fiercely alive, marked by a sharp, unerring eye for detail and a wonderful way with metaphors."

—*The Toronto Star*

"Barnes brings . . . a deceptively relaxed precision and a grown-up acceptance of puzzlement as a natural state of mind."

—*Bonnie Burnard*

CR

Also by Mike Barnes

POETRY

Calm Jazz Sea
(Brick, 1996)

A Thaw Foretold
(Biblioasis, 2006)

SHORT FICTION

Aquarium
(Porcupine's Quill, 1999)

Contrary Angel
(Porcupine's Quill, 2004)

NOVELS

The Syllabus
(Porcupine's Quill, 2002)

Catalogue Raisonné
(Biblioasis, 2005)

THE LILY POND:

A Memoir of Madness, Memory, Myth and Metamorphosis

THE LILY POND

A Memoir of Madness, Memory, Myth and Metamorphosis

MIKE BARNES

BIBLIOASIS

FIRST EDITION

Library and Archives Canada Cataloguing in Publication

Barnes, Mike, 1955–
        The lily pond : a memoir of madness, memory, myth and
metamorphosis / Mike Barnes.

ISBN 10: 1-897231-48-2
ISBN 13: 978-1-897231-48-7

        1. Barnes, Mike, 1955–. 2. Manic-depressive persons—
Canada—Biography.

I. Title.

PS8553.A76332465 2008   616.89'50092   2008-903986-6

Cover design by Heather R. Simcoe.
Readied for the Press by Daniel Wells.

PRINTED AND BOUND IN CANADA

Contents

Two Rooms

How much of our lives happens while we are unconscious? Our life on Earth begins in a room where two bodies lie cooling after love, and our afterlife, whatever it may be, begins in a room where our own body lies cooling after death. In olden times the same room often served for entrance and for exit, a carapace of walls and floor and ceiling that was tenanted and then discarded like the shell borrowed by a wandering hermit crab. Between the chambers housing zygote and corpse comes a succession of rooms in which decisions and actions will be taken that will gratify or thwart our every desire, and in which we will be wholly or partly absent: asleep (up to a third of the time); dozing or preoccupied; misdirected (by a legion of sleight-of-hand artists, ourselves foremost among them); confused, bewildered; or actually gone, two feet or two oceans away from where our fates are being decided by forces and persons who do not need to know, much less consider, our wishes in order to have their way with us. And the way they have with us, which will become in part our way, may be of direct concern to them, but more often and less flatteringly, it will be an indirect consequence, a side issue at best.

ↇ In the late fall of 1978, as I slowly overdosed on the neuroleptic drug Mellaril, I was slipping by steady degrees out of my life. I knew I was being erased—*I'm dying* was a frequent thought, a flat inner admission of the obvious—but the era-sure was by then too far advanced for me to care deeply about it. Only rarely did an awareness that was poignant, abstracted—as if looking at the little that remained of my life from a perspective that had already left it behind—rise to a brief panicked sensation, a flutter by wings incapable of flapping let alone flight. I was more frightened by my in-creasing shortness of breath, an awareness of shallow breathing that crept up on me until I gasped suddenly and gulped in air, though this hardly relieved the sense that I was suffocating. I had always had a horror of being smoth-ered, and I felt now as if someone were pressing a pillow to my face, bringing me repeatedly to the point of blackout, and then easing up a second. If that interval of half-life, shading down to non-life, were to be rendered by a painter, it could only be one of Turner's fogscapes, I think (or one of the similar nocturnes by Whistler), with walls of solid-seeming whitish or grayish vapor shifting sluggishly, and only the vaguest hint here and there, brief dabs of pigment, brush-tip smears in the wet oil, of what might be a bridge, boat, sun. Nothing looming, ever. But shadows occasionally insinuating themselves behind the mists, like the hollows and planes of a face nearing a veil of watered silk. Oblivion, and states approaching it, slide away most determinedly from the very conscious act of writing.

Two images occur to me when I think back on that time, both right in one way and wrong in another.

A candle dwindling down to its final stub. It will soon go out, but for now, the flame around the wick still flickers. That—sufficiency during depletion, up to the puff of extinc-tion—is the wrong part.

The infant Achilles being dipped by his mother into the river Styx. This, surprisingly, is a little better, though still flawed because in my case strength and weakness both came from my immersion in black water, rather than the weakness coming from the small part of me that remained up in the sun, gripped by a mother's hand. Or perhaps that is too shallow a reading of the myth, since Achilles surely suffered as much, and made others suffer, from his invincibility as from his vulnerable heel.

At any rate, during the time of my own lowering, I did in fact spend about an hour out of every twenty-four in the sun with my mother.

About two or three each afternoon, I made my way slowly downstairs and spent up to an hour sitting in the family room in the green swivel armchair that now, almost thirty years after these events, sits in my own apartment as my reading chair. I blinked at familiar sights in the pale light of the northern sun nearing its winter solstice, thinking no thoughts I can remember, perhaps not thinking anything at all, but just sitting there, nominally awake. Mom prepared a small plate of food for me, which I ate without real appetite. Barely eating but always sleeping, and with the water bloat of the drugs, I was gaining weight steadily, a full forty-five pounds above my pre-hospital-admission weight. Pictures of me from that time show a man not just fat in the middle but stretched all over, bloated by edema. My face swelled round, my eyes slitted in watery flesh. Someone I met months later, when the drug was already receding, said my arms looked like clubs. Bland bats: long, smooth, round, heavy. The fluid pooling between my cells was replacing me with one of those segmented dolls used for back pain commercials and car-crash experiments, whose bodies are a series of joined ovals threaded by elastic strings to make them movable. I remember the TV flickering sometimes. I would not have crossed the room to turn it on, but Mom might have done so, in the hope of stimulating or distracting me, or distracting herself from the soft statue of a (briefly) seated man her first child had become. (*Statue*, though it certainly can be lumpish or soft or soft-looking, carries chiselled connotations, hard materials that don't fit; I see more a giant grub, or larva, in my pale soft fleshiness, sluggish rotations under a cocoon of covers, and once-a-day inchings to a nearby feeding.) I see Mom sitting on the matching green loveseat, knitting, but the image flickers less reliably than the remembered television, so perhaps comes only from the undemanding company I have known her to offer, to myself and to other unwell people, on innumerable occasions. She must often have been busy in the kitchen behind me, getting a start on dinner for the four other people who still lived in the house, none of whom I saw anymore. After about forty-five minutes of sitting, I would be falling asleep in the chair, my eyelids dropping heavily, my head lolling above my chest. My hour of consciousness was up. I trudged back upstairs, feeling the strain on each step as atrophied muscles lugged their increased load, went down the hall that after a dim solstitial lightening was again near dark, entered the room at the end of the hall, in which a light never needed to be turned on, and sitting on the edge of the bed removed slowly and with great effort (the slow gropes and plucks of fingers at buttons, the pushing as if at cart wheels stuck in mud of jeans over inflated thighs) all or some of the clothes put on with equal effort an hour before, toppled sideways onto the pillow like a pale tree felled in a swamp, squirmed the still-warm covers around me, and was instantly asleep.

℘ This waning into coma, for which *half-life* is several times too generous a term, was the final phase (or so I assumed at the time) of a long process of extinction that had begun

14

more than a year before with my admission to a hospital under the diagnosis of acute schizophrenia. (Many years later, one of the initial doctors, whom I had begun seeing again, said flatly that this diagnosis had been wrong—the correct one, he said, was bipolar affective disorder, or manic depression as it used to be called—but that the mistake was understandable given the constellation of symptoms I had presented and the kind of violence I had inflicted on myself.) It was a protracted death struggle, made longer by spells and seizures of false hope, of whose main contours and episodes I remained, fittingly for one nearing oblivion, oblivious. Like the personified evening in a poem, "etherised upon a table"—or actually anaesthetized, as will emerge shortly—I sometimes drifted unexpectedly awake, glimpsed lurid and ghastly things, and then sank under again. My scant if piercing memories of that time seem to capture it less well than the myriad unanswered questions that surround them. These questions might be like the negative space that defines a picture, the untouched sections of a woodcut that will take black ink and let the cut-away design show white. (For some reason I think here of Goya's *Head of a Dog*, one of the so-called *pinturas negras*, the black paintings of his old age, found, after his death, painted on the walls of the Quinta del Sordo, the Deaf Man's House, in which the features of the swimming animal are barely separable from the vast dark brown ocean that threatens to—that will soon—engulf him.) But the black space is too large, the questions that comprise it too many. I could not begin to list them. And each question contains another, and that another, like Russian dolls multiplying the unknown. Two doll queries about this final Mellaril room, in which even questions vanished into sleep, will have to stand for all the rest.

Where were the other members of my family? What were they doing? I have to account for them by guesses and surmises. Sue, two years younger than I, whose old room I slept in, was attending York University; I had been living with her and a friend the night I hurt myself. Chris, the middle child of the family, must have been away at school too; he would have been somewhere in his sciences program before entering medical school. That left, besides Mom and Dad, Greg and Sarah still living at home, Greg near the end and Sarah nearer the beginning of high school. I no longer saw them. Not since the early stages of Mellaril, when I would get up periodically and come groggily downstairs for a short spell. Keeping daytime hours, like my father, a busy surgeon, they would leave the house and accomplish their day and return at night all while I was asleep, missing my one-hour sortie into consciousness. I have no idea what they made of my closed door and the silence behind it, which could hardly have been more complete had I been actually dead. Though after many years we are able to speak more freely of the time I was sick, and they show interest and concern when the old symptoms revisit me, I do not really know what they thought or felt when I was vanishing in their midst. They might have fit it all under the rubric of "the illness"—I had heard even senior psychiatrists do the same—and, of course, as a crude approximation, that would not be wrong.

Someone at any rate, I think again it was Mom, called in Dr. Bethune, our long-time family physician, to examine me. He had not, to my knowledge, been consulted previously about a case that was in the hands of specialists. I remember him making what seemed even at that time an old-fashioned house call, perhaps as a favour to old friends. I remember sitting slumped on the edge of the bed, the comforting cold disk of the stethoscope against my chest. I remember his scuffed, black doctor's bag. And I remember clearly him saying, "He's going toxic." It is hard to credit that memory, since it seems bound to have led to a changed course of action, but I can see and hear him saying the words. It would eventually emerge—but when?—that a mistake had been made, and I was on twice the dosage of Mellaril that had been prescribed. But that could not have been clear, or at any rate acted upon, at the time of that bedroom examination, because my slide into coma continued. What happened after I was visited by Dr. Bethune? Did anything happen? I still have nothing but questions.

CR The emergency staff of North York General Hospital could not have had much more than questions on the morning of November 11, 1977, when a twenty-two-year-old white male, agreeably calm and strangely articulate, presented with a deep transverse incision in his belly and shorter slashes across his abdomen and above his left knee. The main wound was of the size and in the place that a later examiner would ask about the patient's appendectomy, and the patient himself spoke wryly of his "self-Caesarean," adding that he guessed it was "in the wrong direction." He also produced a thick hardbound book with a pebbly red cover, which contained some two hundred pages of close-packed writing alternating with drawings and collages, the artwork garishly coloured and badly smeared in places from the artist's taste for thickly applied oil pastels. An interviewer, glancing from time to time up at the patient, riffled through the massed output, too quickly to take in more than an impression of frantic copiousness; the crucially telling point that the book had been new and empty a week before probably did not emerge. I sometimes wonder about those first examiners, whose faces I cannot remember. Where are they now? What are they doing? If still alive, the oldest would be long retired, in advanced old age; the very youngest, residents then, would be in the latter third of a career in medicine. It was twenty-eight years ago, longer than the life of Keats. But whoever they were, and whatever little they had to go on, one thing was certain: they had to do something. The stitching up must have been in some sense soothing to both patient and practitioner: here, at least, was an unquestioned good. An obvious need fitly addressed. Now what?

After I was transferred to Saint Joseph's Hospital in my hometown of Hamilton, the long siege of successive treatments—begun, endured, discarded—commenced. The names of the drugs have the onrushing syllables of the names of warrior kings recited in a foreign epic: Chlorpromazine (Largactil), Cogentin, Haldol (Haloperidol), Stelazine, Mellaril. The primary and secondary effects of all these drugs on me were disastrous. When I wasn't a literally drooling zombie, without the wit to close my mouth when saliva pooled in it, then I was a frantic one beset by an all-over restlessness, an inner itching so relentless that I pounded and pulled and tore at every inch of my skin to try to crush the insects I felt teeming beneath it. I rocked and clutched myself; I paced back and forth along the halls in search of exhaustion; I spun in tight circles like a dog chasing its tail; once, I held myself in standing push-up position, hands spread flat against the wall, and drove my forehead repeatedly into the plaster until I collapsed in blackness. The meaning of neuroleptic, "nerve seizing," captures the semi-paralysing effect the phenothiazine drugs have on the brain and nervous system but also, in my experience, the way they stop the normally fluent processes of perception and cognition, make them catch and grind like rusty gears. Events and objects lost their discrete stops and starts; they jerked and wavered, as if seen in stop-time or phase shifts, like film stock with damaged celluloid and missing frames. Edges and outlines were not only blurred but hideously furred, as if the world and everything in it had grown a pelt. This applied equally to a large view and a small one: a table, a face, a button—all had a fringed circumference, a hairy halo like rug fibres seen from close up, that at times seemed more spine-like, sharp little spikes sticking out in all directions. This, of course, was obnoxious and revolting; and the worst part of the distortion was its fractal nature, by which the same sights insisted on themselves at any segment or scale, which made for an effect of infinite ugliness, a world of monstrous monotony, whose most monstrously monotonous aspect was its endlessly replicated uniformity.

At some point in this siege, well past the start but before Mellaril, I began to visit a room near the meds station. The Treatment Room, so named by a small sign on the adjoining wall, was the room beyond two wide metal doors that swung inward and normally stayed locked except for an hour or so each morning, and it was where I received my electroconvulsive therapy, or ECT. Some of my drug trials, the doctors all but admitted, had been shots in the dark—or shots at the dark—temporizing tactics in an intractable case that was bewildering and frustrating for all concerned. ECT was different. From the start someone had conceived it as a determined push that would be seen through to the end. Numbers were strongly associated with the process: I was to receive several series, each consisting of a number of individual treatments grouped closely together (Monday, Wednesday, Thursday, I seem to recall), with slightly longer pauses between one series and the next. Several treatments made up one series; several series made up the course; I think now that was how it worked. Reactions to treatments and series would be noted, of course, but an overall assessment of the effectiveness of electroshock would be deferred until completion of the entirety. Whatever rationale was given then for persisting in such quantities of ECT, I mostly see it now as a drastic measure taken for want of a better plan. This view is supported by a clear memory I have from this time, the hopeless middle of the campaign, of a conversation with a senior psychiatrist in which he told me that he had resisted the general consensus at a staff meeting that I be transferred to the Ontario Hospital on the "mountain" (Hamilton's escarpment) for long-term care, a relocation known among the patients as "bagging." (We reacted to someone's bagging as herd animals might to a cull, dispersing to our rooms when the relocators came, or, if trapped in the open, clustering in corners as distant as possible, where we chatted far more convivially than was usual, signing to the visitors that we had nothing in common with the meek and depleted-looking entity they were escorting to the elevator.) Rightly or wrongly—that is, as paranoid delusion or realistic fear—I understood this deferral of my bagging to be conditional on my acceptance of whatever even more rigorous measures might be necessary to alter my condition.

It is time, now, to re-enter the room of ECT—yet still I find myself hanging back. Before returning there, which involves a kind of bagging too, I have to resort to the temporizing course of a few more sentences. Recently, when my wife, Heather, and I were having dinner with friends, the talk turned late at night, over glasses of red wine, to the very vivid and tactile memories two of them had from all periods of their lives, which gave them a strong connection to their earlier selves and a feeling that they could freely access, if not all, then at least a great deal of the continuous memory track we are said to be making of our ongoing experiences. We were all struck by the contrast between this and my own account of memory. It consisted, I said, of brief scenes or tableaux, or details from these, popping out of patches of fog, patches that were so lengthy at times that the clear fragments stood starkly isolated between them, with guesswork and invention needed to construct a context in which they might have occurred. I said that writing strengthened my sense of continuity, both, I think—and it is very hard to know which process is occurring when, or to what degree they overlap and intertwine—by aiding my recall, helping to pull out fragments I didn't know were there, and also by creating plausible fragments to fill in the gaps in a scene. The obliterating fog is more extensive the further I go into the past, but it covers large sections of recent time too; I have the sense sometimes that I am staying just ahead of it, so to speak, stepping out from it to stare, alert and surprised, at the present I find myself in. Crusoe mode, as Heather and I call this islanding in the present, has its positive aspect. Washed up on a new beach, you focus intently on the things about you: grains of sand, a shell, the leaves of a new tree, a footprint. You are alive to the life about you in a way you scarcely could have been during the routine and tedium of the voyage. But then Crusoe has keen memories, scenes that flock to haunt and depress him, of his life before his stranding, so the analogy cannot be pushed too far. One of our friends asked Heather afterward if I thought my long-ago ECT treatments had affected my memory. I have no answer for this. Certainly the likelihood of short-term memory loss was stressed; it was virtually guaranteed, the doctors warned, but so was the fact that in the majority of cases the loss would be transient, with any remaining blank spots confined to the times around the treatments themselves. So I have no way of knowing what part the multiple series of ECT treatments, combined with the various neuroleptic drugs, play in the more general amnesia that I find writing, among its other attractions, a partial antidote for, though it seems to me unlikely that there would not be some lasting changes brought about by so many chemical and electrical jolts to the brain, especially as these produced other, also unexplained, effects, some of which lasted for years after my eventual discharge. For a long time, when I masturbated, which I only slowly recovered the energy and inclination to do, my orgasm, when I could achieve it at all, was strangely faint, a mild, faraway-seeming spasm that was also completely dry. Even later when the climax gained in intensity, causing me to seek it more regularly, not one drop of semen was ejaculated. I would pass my fingers over my belly in amazement, mystified by this fundamental change in my body. Did it mean I was now sterile? (The crack-brained narrator of a blackly comic novel I wrote many versions of, beginning around 1992, pens a poem entitled "The Mad Mule.") This state of things lasted for about two years, long enough that I was startled one night when a single drop of ejaculate leaked out of me. Since then I have functioned normally, and I have never heard or read any explanation for my arid interval. A much longer-lasting and more worrisome symptom was the seizure-like shudderings, occurring at first many times daily, during which my whole body would stiffen suddenly, my muscles clenching in a rigid spasm—more like an orgasm, it occurs to me now, than my actual climax, though devoid of pleasure and frightening in its intensity and sudden onset. The rigidity would last a second or two and then relax. This could occur without warning at any time of day and could vary in intensity and duration, though the occurrences were more frequent and more intense at night. These abrupt stiffenings were something like the myoclonic jerks that can come before sleep, but they were stronger and more long-lasting and not confined to times when I was near sleep or even sleepy. The experience of seizing up from head to toe in this way made me feel that my nervous system had slipped a cog, like a faulty clock whose hand will tick regularly, then freeze quivering for a moment before jumping to the next numeral. I was seeing no psychiatrists by then—I found and kept finding ways to get by outside the hospital system for a full ten years—but when I was again forced, by a particularly severe crisis and the lack of a better alternative, to consult a physician, I mentioned these seizure-like events, which had abated but never entirely ceased, and the doctor had me tested for epilepsy. The results came back negative.

Now, at last, I think I am ready to venture back into the ECT room. There is not much to tell, which is perhaps precisely why I delayed so long in telling it. Incredibly to me, now that I am faced with it again, I find that there was even more to say about the foggy descent under Mellaril than about the brief repeated void of ECT, which consisted of no more, beforehand, than a moment of porcelain poise under bright white lights and hovering faces, and afterward, a bewildered gathering of shards. In between was nothing I knew. Each time I entered the ECT room, I prepared myself as best I could for extinction, and my preparation was never in vain. In both rooms, Mellaril and ECT, I died and was reborn, but in ECT the death was instantaneous and repeated, many deaths, and the rebirth on the other side was not only of someone I could not be sure was me, but of something I could not be sure was a person. Partly this must have been due to memory loss and disruption, which shattered the continuity between past and present. But also, the ritual aspect of ECT, with the patient's voluntary offering of himself for therapeutic oblivion, is not concordant with an expectation of renewed or even continued life: one does not lie down on a stone slab expecting to re-emerge in this world. The old snake-pit melodramas are condemned now for the cruelties they depict and, perhaps, exaggerate, but watching them one never lost the sense that the raving inmate wrestled to the floor by brutal attendants was one with the subdued person who had been straightjacketed or injected or strapped down or locked in. The focus on resistance hardly overcome—a screaming mouth plugged with rubber, eyes furious until closed, limbs punching and kicking until pinned—reassured, in perhaps the genre's most sentimental gesture, the persistence of identity through resistance. I did not resist. I presented myself at the double doors at 8:00 a.m. I answered no to the question of whether I had had anything to eat or drink since midnight. No, not even water, I said. Was I sure? Yes. A strange part of the ritual was the stretcher covered with a white sheet and with a pillow on it that poked out into the hall after the double doors had opened. On the surface it seems bizarre to use a stretcher to transport an ambulatory patient a few feet to the treatment table where he will lie down. But I think now that the stretcher was a prudent guarantee that the patient's acquiescence would not falter at a clear view of the table and the machines and equipment surrounding it. Supine on the stretcher, one could not help but return in part to the luxuriant helplessness of the infant's perspective, with its straight-up view of a bland sky-ceiling bobbing with familiar moon faces. All else is peripheral blurs, or, if the head turns either way, mere fragments, bits and parts of things. The world telescoped or magnified, which is not the world an adult moves through and must act upon. A brief ride, a little glide on wheels, and then hands are helping me slide from one surface to another harder and cooler one.

White lights—fuzzy stars when my glasses are removed. A brief silence, and then the anaesthetist takes his seat on the stool. He is just above my level. He takes my hand in his hand, cool and firm. "Little prick," he says and slides his needle beneath the skin and then tapes it down. I have fought the flurries in my stomach, the rituals have helped; I have no beliefs, but I feel that it is bad to go out screaming; but now, at last, it is hard not to scream. All the homely smallnesses and the murmuring familiars fall away, and I realize that I am here, and that I am here alone. A coldness that has something of peppermint about it, a dry cold that hovers on the edge of smell and taste, creeps up from the base of my spine with such seeming slowness that I am urging it upward before my self-control collapses, then blooms in a sweetish vapor that fills my sinuses and the back of my throat, and it is then, smelling and tasting something I cannot describe and will never forget, something wholly artificial that resembles many smells and tastes without being any of them, that I have a split second of perfect and utterly terrifying lucidity, in which I know that I am being jammed head downward into dirt. That is the last thing I know.

I have wondered sometimes at the curious word *abjection*, which seems to combine so perfectly *absent* (or *absence*) and *object* (or *objection*). For it seems often to be the case that to become, or to endure becoming, an object, you have to go away from your life, you have to vacate it of your will so that another will can occupy it, and, on the other side, when you are absent from your life you become a room for rent or purchase or, at the extreme, a space for squatter's rights. Abjection. The question is whether your abjection, which may be felt as an offense by yourself or others, can rise to the active status of an objection. It will mean inserting parentheses into the equation of surrender, placing the copula verb in a kind of grammatical womb to reserve for consciousness its proper scope and efficacy: I (am) object.

Next I see dirty orange with fibres coming out of it. My stomach lurches, and I shut my eyes so as not to throw up. For a long time I keep tumbling back down into sleep, and I am grateful for this, because all I can see, every time my eyes roll open, is more of the fuzzy orange mixed with other unpleasant colours, dull lime and muddy pink, all with the spiky and fringed fibres criss-crossing every which way, like magnified hairs or insect legs. Even when I come awake a little more and move my head slightly, I see only these lurid, sickening sights. As if the place I am in is nothing but a giant hairball with a background of drying secretions. I feel groggy, nauseous. I am so confused that I am not even sure of the orientation of my body. I am a while, for instance, realizing that I am lying on my side on a couch. The cool, smoother thing my cheek rests on is my arm. After more "a whiles"—with no sense of time at all, except as a kind of small history beginning, an inventory of the things discovered in the previous whiles: couch, body, arm, carpet—I realize that I am waking from sleep in a small alcove. No idea how I came to be in this place. I hear sounds and move my head enough to see people's legs going by. My hand goes to my temple and finds something dry, flaky there. When I pull a bit away, it looks like the whitish flakes of dried glue or semen. Someone has come on my head? I raise my head slightly; the room whirls, and I come close to throwing up again, but I find more flakes on the other temple before I collapse back down on my arm. None of it makes any sense to me. I can't fit these fragments together, and I feel sicker when I try. Like someone with the flu trying to fit a jigsaw puzzle together with most of the pieces missing. Footsteps approach, and there is a woman nearby; I can smell her perfume. I keep my eyes closed. She goes away. A few such visits later, I feel her closer than before; I sense she will not leave this time, and I slit my eyes and see hairy columns, brown pant legs, a few inches away. Nausea; I shut my eyes. But she stays, and so I try to raise myself. It is difficult: not only is the whirling worse with my head up, but I feel so utterly exhausted, my arms weak and trembly despite their thick appearance, every molecule in my body a stone dragging me down. "Groggy . . . woozy . . . so heavy," I hear myself saying in answer to her questions. The words surprise me. They seem like lucky finds, helium balloons whose strings I have found drifting in hairy space. After a time I find two more: "What happened?" "You had ECT two hours ago," she says in a kind, calm tone, as if she was prepared for this question and is not dismayed by it. It is the tone I trust rather than the answer, which I don't understand. Soon I will look up from her pants and scuffed white shoes to see her face, if she has a face. Eventually I will even link my arm through hers and wander dazedly along the hall, wondering at what the faces and objects I am seeing might mean, and what could possibly be my place among them.

Sometime after the entire course of ECT was completed, I was started on Mellaril, one of the few remaining phenothiazines I had not yet taken.

ℭℜ Early on, when there were brief periods of waking between sleeps, my eyes rolling open for a few minutes and then drooping shut again, I would stare at the leafless branches of the crabapple tree just beyond the window in my sister's room. The black limbs were starkly outlined against the pale gray sky; when damp, especially, they had a greasy vividness, like the tracings of a lithographer's pencil on his prepared limestone. Their spidery elegance filled the square of window entirely, extending beyond it, so that I was conscious of looking at a section of a cropped picture, a part of the traceries or fretwork of a much larger structure, like the intricate wrought-iron struts of some massive architecture in which my borrowed room hung. Now, from this vantage point, I imagine the dense and impassable brier hedge encasing Sleeping Beauty, a comparison which seems apt in some ways but which could not have occurred to me then, since it requires resources of memory and hope I could not have summoned. I did not then have an imagination as I know it now and as I had known it before. My own brain had become an alien and sickening power to me. I had hidden from its relentless churning when I could, endured it when I could not escape. Even delicate things, like the thin and tapering branches, it turned brute and gigantic. Overwhelming structures and machines, things of crushing immensity and power, and the incessant and unfathomable whirlings of their innumerable wheels and gears—constant impressions of this kind, which I saw everywhere I looked, produced a queasy revulsion, a nausea without the relief of vomiting. It had an analogue in my earlier experience, of being a tiny child simultaneously mesmerized and sickened by spinning and thrashing amusement park rides. The drugs made this worse, but they also clouded and slowed all mental operations, including the worst ones. Horror and sleep made a pact at a level that was, finally, below nightmare: I and the world would become inorganic at the same rate and to the same end, like a supersaturated solution to which the seed has been added, crystal joining to crystal inside and out.

Before this pact was finalized under the reign of Mellaril, however, there were some awful moments to endure. The sight of the first snow covering the ground struck me with the finality of a coffin lid, since I knew that the world it covered would not be returning, at least not to my eyes. It melted, and the damp ground was restored, but I knew that soon the whiting out would be complete and, in my case, irreversible. This was winter as I, twenty-three, had never known it before: winter stripped to its essentials, frozen and absolute. A shudder shook me repeatedly to think I would not see the ground again—the bare ground, that simplest of things—and that the round of seasons I had known for ninety-three turns was stopping on this sliver of ice. The glitter and intricacy of snowflakes, which had delighted me before, now gave me the horrors. Snow became the sinister frosting on a toxic cake, a gloating, white shimmer. It was the universal shroud, that master of ultimate discretion that would seal away a world and slide it into the deep freeze. But soon the queasy terror I felt at effacement was itself effaced, buried under a torpor that let through fewer and fewer vestiges of thought and feeling. As always it was the transition, the in-between zone, that was hardest. It was the flayed nerves of the death-row wait that made one flee into collaboration with the executioner, seeing the room at the end of the hall first with grim resignation and then with frigid longing.

℞ But there are rooms within rooms—closets, cupboards, locked compartments—and in one of these a spark of gold may flash counter to the general deadening. These treasure chests must remain so deeply sunk that the always more or less entrepreneurial life at the surface can never find them. They can dispense life-saving coin while safeguarding the hoard.

One evening near Christmas I awoke around 8:00 p.m., a time of day during which I had not been conscious for weeks, a time when I would normally have been several hours into my twenty-three-hour sleep. I was beyond any reckoning of time, and there was no clock or calendar in the room (had someone removed them?), but I heard, from downstairs, the after-dinner sounds of my family, who in those days ate late and retired early, and I saw Christmas lights twinkling on the trees and houses on the drive to the hospital a short time later. *Elves' eyes*, I remember thinking of the small, bright colours glowing and blinking from within dark branches. It may have been the first clear thought —other than *I'm dying*—that I had had in weeks. For some reason, which may be only a retroactive desire for symmetry, I think it was actually between the holidays, closer to New Year's. I have no memory I can trust of actually cutting my wrist—the Hamlet pause before the mirror, the sight from the small bathroom window of snow-shrouded streets below, the second pause with razor above upturned arm: these are only what any competent scene-filler would insert, and they have a grainy, ad hoc feel about them. What I do remember distinctly are the bright red droplets springing in a row out of white, like red berries popping up out of snow. That and—this is trustworthy though muffled, because the events themselves were muffled, the actions fumbly and the few words mumbled—coming out of the bathroom next to my room and seeing my parents coming down the dim hall (no light on yet; there hadn't been one needed there for so long), who must have heard the unaccustomed sounds above their heads just as I had heard the accustomed ones from below. Or perhaps, on that particular evening, something just nudged or whispered them upstairs, as I had been nudged or whispered awake, and they moved along with me in obedience to it. There was that sense of following a dream choreography, where the movements are strange but purposeful and coordinated.

The wound was not life-threatening: it was not a suicide attempt. But it was not negligible either: a quarter century later, the white lines still declare themselves plainly across the underside of my left wrist, just below my hand, with two curious semicircles of white dots above and below them (the stitches were left in too long, and the skin pulled away from the threads), the whole pattern of complementary curves and midline suggesting, roughly, the outline of two full lips pressed tight in concentration. The act seems—amazingly, considering the fogbound, almost vanished creature who produced it—well-calibrated. An act of desperation, certainly, but as well a determined and even agile grab at life by a far stronger, far more resourceful person than I seemed capable of being. That must be, too, along with the drug haze, why my actions seemed so unreal, so groggily fantastic, as I committed them. Being wholly incapable of acting on my own behalf, and close to incapable of acting at all, I had to take direction from someone else, inside myself and yet beyond myself—someone who wanted me to live and saw a way, crude on the surface but perhaps precisely wrought, to shove a near-corpse through a fast-closing door.

I remember no alarm, no sadness. No grim satisfaction, either. I was below such reactions, in a state so close to paralysis, it would need to rise several large degrees even to reach the mobility of tears. For this reason psychiatric literature warns that suicide is of greatest danger as severely depressed patients are emerging from their depressions: it is the long steep passage down into or up out of the underworld that is most perilous. I enacted what was necessary on autopilot, absently and efficiently. Nor do I remember alarm on the part of my parents as I approached them with the evidence outstretched, like a man whose broken pact with death consists precisely in his renewed willingness to harm himself. We were all, it seems to me, in thrall to someone who knew better. Dazed and damaged by our fourteen-month ordeal, we recognized and were grateful for the face of a new imperative: a hand offering a thread out of the maze.

On the suicide ward, two floors below 4A, one of the first procedures was to stop all previous meds. In almost all cases a heavy course of antidepressants, at least, would soon be reapplied, but first there was this clean-slate protocol: to reduce in number the forces contending for the one who had tried to reduce himself to zero. Slowly, in tiny increments but beginning almost immediately, I began to feel better. One of the first signs was my looking around me at the other suicide survivors—the blade-slit, rope-burned, leap-fractured, drug-bleared, powder-singed—each scarred by the double stigmata of both attempt and deferral: bandages, neck braces, casts, IV bags and poles—and thinking (in these words or something close to them) *I'm not one of you.* Non-fellowship was a first small step out of hell. And, though welcome, it came with its own queer twist of sadness and shame. And guilt: some people, even there, were garrulous, but I couldn't talk to them on an even footing and felt false trying. *I don't belong here.*

With fresh hope came a new fear, an anxiety that someone would ignore the evidence, which was still slow-growing and far from obvious, that I was coming around and start me on another drug routinely. I had so small a purchase on recovery—I was no more than grazing the lip of it—that if someone had handed me new pills, I doubted my powers to refuse or even to postpone taking them. Luckily—almost miraculously, it seems to me now—no one did. Someone had the sense to stand back for the moment and let things be.

The pause—the first real pause in fourteen months—continued. Little by little I felt better. Bit by bit I returned toward myself. On Ward 2, and on Ward 4A when they moved me upstairs, I tried to project an aura, not of invisibility, for disappearance would provoke search parties, but of boring visibility, of unremarkable recovery. If I can only continue falling through the cracks, I thought, or sensed without thinking, as an animal always knows intuitively where its best chances lie, my parachute will—or can, or might—open between this cage and the ground. When I could not avoid passing the meds nurse and her station, I fought the urge to slouch or creep and instead walked forthrightly, at a moderately brisk pace, as if I had some ordinary business at the other end of the hall. In this way, over a third of a year, I saw what I had not expected to see again, not only the full extent of winter but, beyond it, spring.

ભ Zeno, a philosopher of the Eleatic school in the fifth century BC, developed several ingenious paradoxes to show the logical impossibility, and thus the illusoriness, of motion and plurality. In his most famous paradox, Achilles runs a footrace against a tortoise. The tortoise, crucially, is allowed a head start. But Achilles, for all his speed, cannot catch the tortoise: as the hero runs a hundred yards to where the tortoise started, the tortoise has plodded ten yards; when Achilles closes that ten yards, the tortoise has managed one; another yard for Achilles, another tenth of a yard for the tortoise . . . and so on. Achilles can never quite catch his adversary, who stays always fractionally ahead of him. Interestingly, if you reverse the starting positions of the racers, the paradox disappears, but it is replaced by another one (which is perhaps more rueful irony than paradox): now Achilles has no trouble outrunning the tortoise—darting ten yards while the tortoise plods one, he quickly increases the distance between them—yet he can never be said to have finally, once and for all, escaped his pursuer, who continues doggedly approaching no matter how vast the gap between them grows. In fact, if Achilles pauses to rest for an instant, as even heroes may be supposed to do, then he may feel a queasy sense, to paraphrase a more recent riddler, that something is gaining on him. And in this apprehension he will always be correct.

Hunters in the Snow

There is a story I have never been able to write. My many attempts to write it, over the course of more than thirty years, filled a large trunk with notebooks and loose papers and called on every tactic of the writing life I knew: notes, outlines, charts, diagrams, sketches of scenes and characters, drafts of lengthy episodes from multiple slants and viewpoints, more notes, memos, maps, checklists, deadlines, ideas for possible endings. All of these pushes petered out. That should have been enough, usually it would have been, to convince me that if there was in fact a story there, it was not one I could find or force into being. Normally that is when the impulse would begin to fade, its claims on my energies, if not revealed as spurious, at least worn down by attrition. It could hang in that dim and musty closet with all the other might-have-beens. But this one stayed. I would see its fragments vividly—surrounded by a bright, even light that gave them a theatrical grandeur—and they seemed so luminous as to be complete in themselves, except that I could feel their connectedness—these invisible lines radiating out from them—to other scenes and people speaking, some I could glimpse, some I could just sense hulking out there, like shapes in the night beyond the range of a campfire. They carried that imperative charge: *Me.* Which, if you have heard it before, cannot be mistaken for *This might be fun* or *That could work*. But when something has been giving you notice of itself for many years, while just as persistently resisting your attempts either to drag it into being or give it a decent burial—it drains you. You gain a fuller understanding of the human obsession with vampires, which are a fact of daily life we all cope with, and you wonder if the "undead" could not with as much precision be called the "unalive." And the thought occurs, it has to at some point: Maybe partway's all this one's willing to come. It has seed that fertilizes, develops to a point—but it can't grow all the way into independent life. Acceptance of that—call it wisdom or resignation or tiredness, or the borderland where those familiars shake hands in a pact—can come creeping over you, try to put down roots. It never feels right or good, just tolerable. There's a ghost in your attic that shuffles and creaks—it won't leave, but it won't insist on further entry into your world. You can live with that, you guess. Or you might try one more time to flesh it out.

CR French River, now named a "heritage river" for its part in the early fur trade, with a roadside Visitors' Centre and explanatory plaques telling of Indians and voyageurs and missionaries, runs for about sixty-five miles from Lake Nipissing to Georgian Bay. When the river has completed roughly two thirds of its journey from source to mouth—its present source and mouth; it flowed the other way as recently as ten thousand years ago—its north and main channels, which had separated to go around Eighteen Mile Island, come together again in Dry Pine Bay. About five miles long and a mile wide at its northern end, this roughly egg-shaped body of water is like a big lake; there are vacationers, veterans of many summers, who have never ventured into, and in one extreme case never even heard of, the intricate river system, filled with rapids and waterfalls and near-lying lakes, that spills into this place of confluence, somewhere the river pauses, so to speak, to pool itself before rippling onward. Dry Pine is naturally very deep, up to a hundred and fifty feet in places. My parents built their cottage on a large island on the eastern side of the bay, in 1966, when I was eleven, and one of the most astounding, and rather eerie, memories I have from the few summers I spent there was of being startled by a large splash—this would always happen on a day of baking heat, when the water was glassy and millpond flat—and turning in time (you had to be quick) to see a brown-and-gray shape, the length of a grown man or woman, fall stiffly back into the water with an even louder splash, so loud in the silence that it was like a tree crashing through brush, sending out concentric ripples that were a long time subsiding. "The sturgeon," we always said, as if it was always the same old freshwater leviathan that had propelled itself from murky depths to stand, for an unreal moment, on its tail in glittering sun.

French River has often become "Black River" in the stories I have set there, a name that is apt for the dark colour of its water, but also for the depression and massy-ness that descend upon me when I try to write about it. When I talk to my family about French River it becomes clear, at least to me, that my memories of the region are fewer and more fragmentary, yet at the same time seemingly more dense and fraught, than the ones they cherish. Partly this is due to the very different amounts of time we have spent there. I was at the cottage for eight summers before I left home in my late teens, and since then my visits have been sporadic and brief: a day or two here and there, occasionally a stay of up to a week. I remember, before and after this cottage interlude, summers spent in the city, and holiday trips to other cities and other waterside cabins. Sarah, though, the youngest in the family, has links with French River that reach back to her beginnings; there is a wonderful sun-filled photo of her as a naked smiling child, younger than two, eating a sandwich in a deck chair overlooking Dry Pine Bay. Most years, all of my siblings—Sue, Chris, Greg, and Sarah—vacation at the French. And from the time they built the cottage in their fortieth year, my parents have stayed there for most of every summer, many spring and fall weekends (and one near-fatal winter one), and up to five months a year since my father's retirement. So it is natural that they participate, more actively than I ever could, in the very Canadian practice of making of the cottage an idyll, a place of such magical and benign loveliness that it has the power to erase, and then restore, the supposedly more complex and confused and strife-filled life in the main home in the city. They express surprise when I can't recall this picnic or that fishing trip—and I think I do exaggerate these memory lapses sometimes, just to counter their assumption of a fully shared experience. Sometimes a puzzled or hurt look creeps into their eyes at the casualness I betray about a place they reverence. And, in fact, this casualness is not really true to my own experience, is part shorthand, even part self-betrayal. Certainly I have been touched deeply by the same things that move them: current and wind in competing swirls, the click and snap of aspen leaves, storm clouds building over cliffs, a white curtain of rain rushing down the bay; the tang of pine resin, the butter swoop of a goldfinch, a hundred other things . . . it is just—it is mainly, I think, a difference in our sense of the uniqueness (to French River) of these things, which I have found elsewhere too, and in our sense of proprietorship over them. I have been a sometime tenant—to be sure, often a very glad and grateful one—at French River, just as I am a tenant in the apartment in which I write this.

Two paragraphs ago, I toyed with the idea of describing Dry Pine Bay as the tear duct, or bridge of the nose, at the edge of the huge almond eye made by Eighteen Mile Island and the two channels, or eyelids, going around it. The fancifulness of that, its bird's-eye detachment and irony, captures nicely the difference I am talking about. The true believer does not toy with an icon. Neither does the atheist. Only the agnostic—not fully subscribed, conflicted in his connections—feels the need to fondle irreverently, craving the touch but resisting the grasp.

For my fiftieth birthday party, in August 2005, Heather and I were staying in a cabin we had rented at Meshaw Falls, where the north channel empties into Dry Pine Bay. The party, a family-only affair, was held the day before my birthday down at the south end of the bay, at cabins rented by three of my siblings (Sarah had just moved and could not attend), beside the nine-hole golf course that had been fashioned by a Seagram heir in the 1920s out of an early settler's stony and unproductive farm. The gathering was originally to have taken place at Indian Point—as a faded wooden sign over the door proclaims the family cottage (embarrassingly to me, though it was I, in fact, who painted the sign and sawed its ragged edges, and it is true that Indian families lived on the land in tents and shacks for decades)—but the party as planned was first cancelled and then made provisional but more "low-key," to accommodate both the depression I had been wrestling with for months, a flare-up (which felt like the guttering) of an old condition, and my parents' diminished abilities, as they neared eighty and coped with their own serious health problems, to meet the demands of hosting the event.

As the birthday boy, I was supposed to have been left out of the planning entirely. The right to "just show up" would be my first gift. Inevitably, though, despite everyone's best intentions, I was consulted many times throughout the year, whenever a snag or possible change came up. This even became a family joke, as I protested the arduousness of turning myself fifty, a job that had commenced right after my forty-ninth birthday (or possibly just before it!), and looked forward to the relative ease of merely being fifty. My role in the family had long been clear to everyone: the facilitator, the peacemaker, the linchpin; the hub of the centrifuge that keeps the disparate parts from flying off into space; the glue, invisible or semi-transparent, that holds everything together—and no one commented anymore, if they ever had, on a discrepancy between this role and a psychiatric history stretching back three decades combined with an increasingly reclusive lifestyle. Perhaps there isn't any discrepancy. Once, in a psychiatrist's office, when I mused about the absurdity or paradox in my family role, saying that one would expect such a position to be occupied by the most sane and capable member, the doctor retorted sharply, "Well, you are." It was a rap on the knuckles, matching the look of disapproval on his face—and well-deserved, for we had business too urgent to be fooling with false modesty.

So there were ample pressures, from within and without, to make me dread a little this fiftieth celebration. None, or very little, of it had to do with a fear of actually being fifty. One of the few consolations for unhappy early years is that one is spared the nostalgia most people feel for youth, except as an opportunity lost without ever quite being tried. My late teens and twenties and thirties were so harrowing that, in general, the middle years have proved more comfortable than any earlier stretch. I was touched that my family wanted to celebrate in my honour, but, depressed and depleted as I felt, I tended to view the festivities as a trial I needed to get through, and to some extent bring off, rather than as a moment I could bask in. More millstone than milestone, as I muttered many times to Heather.

It turned out to be a good deal better than that. At least at the start. The adults sat on lawn chairs arranged in a large semicircle, in a clearing where grass turned patchy and then gave way to scuffed and char-blackened dirt around a fireplace of ringed stones. Large birches and aspens and pines stood round the clearing, offering shade but letting through generous shafts and coins of sunlight. Looking out over a parapet of dense bushes, below which stretched a wide, weedy beach, wider and muddier over its riverside third due to water levels of a record lowness, one could see all the way up the huge blue oval of Dry Pine Bay, a pleasant cool breeze rippling down from the north. Drinks and hors d'oeuvres were served; gifts were placed on an empty chair beside me. The clearing and cabin were decorated with balloons and streamers and a pencil-crayoned HAPPY BIRTHDAY poster; speeding down the centre of the bay in our borrowed boat, Heather and I had seen the bright colours pop out from the surrounding foliage, the ring of people waiting in their chairs. Dinner, after the cocktails and gift opening, would consist of thick barbecued steaks, various salads, and my favourite cake from childhood, angel food with white frosting, made by my mother. Sitting near the centre, receiving all this bounty, I felt very moved and nearly mute, able only to murmur repeated soft exclamations and thank you's. All of the decorations and drinks and foods had been bought, and some of them prepared, in far-flung cities and towns, and then driven up to three hundred miles to this clearing in the woods. The gifts showed a cautious creativity and delicate thoughtfulness: an hors d'oeuvres platter and bowl made by a ceramic artist, depicting a birchbark canoe floating on a blue-green lake; a collage of photos culled from family albums, weighted toward French River sun and grins over catches of fish; a digital voice recorder, to make safer and more convenient the copious notes I sometimes scribble in the car, usually but not always while stopped. I felt a tender, chest-squeezing sensation, almost smothering in its intensity, at the anxious hope and rallying-round this party, among its simpler, less commingled pleasures, represented. There were no pictures in the photo collages from the last fifteen years and only two or three from the eighteen years before that. Thirty-three years lay between this late afternoon, slowly dimming now, pooling its shadows toward dusk, and the eldest son and older brother conjured on these bristol boards and construction papers: the bigger, the stronger, the smarter at school; the conqueror and transmitter of firsts; the dresser of cuts and scrapes; the deliverer from bullies and deep water. Unvanquishable, he must have seemed—and apparently still does seem sometimes, uncannily, some core of myth intact despite the more than three decades of precipitous falls and long slow climbs, slides and wily scale-backs, according to some persistence of family memory and personal meaning that I could scarcely credit but only be amazed by, a little frightened at, and above all deeply grateful for. None of this seemed sayable, even obliquely, and except for snatches of catch-up news and a few mild jokes, the party was strangely silent, quite wordless at times, a fact doubly strange in a clan of great talkers, boisterously articulate, at a party thrown for its previously most prolific talker, who had channelled much of his gab into writing but who could still, when not islanded by speechlessness, gush great rivers of stories and debate. They brought things to me, I thought, in something like the hush of hospital visitants: handing over a treat of food or a small remembrance, then watching from nearby with a shy and slightly pained discretion to see if it was, if it still could be, enjoyed.

In the distance off to our right, in the tall grass of the curving beach, the children—one of my two nephews and my two nieces—were hunting frogs with Greg's black Labrador, Ebony. Earlier they had been seated in the circle or playing near it; now they walked and crouched in a slanting, theatrical beam of light that missed the darkening clearing and made us seem, in reality only a hundred yards apart, to be in two different time zones. Their figures in the bright light seemed both removed and immediate, like onstage actors seen from the back of a large theater. They worked soundlessly and as a team: one of them keeping Ebony safely back (they took turns at this), the other two scouting, crouching, pouncing—sometimes cornering a leaping target between them—and then all three examining the captured specimen and letting it go. It looked pointless, absorbing, peaceful. A world away from my own boyhood memories of catching frogs for fishing, with my brothers and my father, when we became as efficient as a frog-catching factory, each of us able to snatch a third frog while pinning another two already caught between closed fingers. The thirty or forty young leopard frogs were kept in a metal minnow bucket with handfuls of leaves and a little water, the popcorn-like pings of their vain leaps at the lid becoming infrequent after the first day (and instantly quelled, anyway, by a sharp rap with the knuckles on the pail, which must have sounded like awesome thunder inside in the dark), amid fetid, excremental smells that grew stronger as their wastes accumulated and the bodies of the first dead ones, often hidden under leaves, began to putrefy. When hooked through the snout, they made terribly human grabs with their tiny hands to try to remove the source of the pain, or else twisted upward suddenly, wrapping their strong back legs around the line like upside-down gymnasts on a rope, trying to relieve the torment of gravity. It had always seemed extravagantly cruel to me, needless if one could accept the slightly diminished angling odds afforded by artificial lures, and I had long ago stopped using, apart from a few instances of collegial cowardice, the "Live Bait" I described in a grisly published poem. But my memories of those frog hunts were strong and shameful. What the kids were doing now seemed, in contrast, serene and humane. I wished I could join them. Not to play with them as a self-consciously benevolent uncle, but simply to walk alongside them, to watch. A day later I would do exactly that, in the same time and place, and it would be so eerily as I had imagined it, that it was as if I had transported myself mentally from the birthday party into the near future, and there had merely been a twenty-four hour delay for my body to catch up to my thought.

After sunset I could see my parents becoming more restless, confused and ill at ease as darkness began to fall —feeling their aches and pains and wanting to get home— and I knew that if I was going to speak it had better be now. With each passing year, more and more of Dad's conversation revolved around his feeling increasingly addled and ailing. What he regretted most acutely, even mourned, he told me, was what he saw as an irrecoverable loss of mental sharpness, which he found even more debilitating than the numerous joint and spinal problems that had required three major surgeries and caused him cruel pain. Never a sociable man, he now disliked more than ever leaving the house, preferring to stick to the routines he and Mom had long ago established, and welcoming only occasional family visitors, preferably one at a time. In me, his most frequent confidant, he valued, he told me often with misting eyes, not only my empathy and patience but also my relative youth and health which lifted his spirits to witness. Though moved close to tears myself by his words, I was also puzzled by them, since to sustain this image of a thriving son he had to forget, at least momentarily, what to me was unforgettable: my long history of paralyzing depressions, which left me little mental functioning above the autonomic level, and, at the other pole, the frenzied manias that had shredded rational judgement (and this only on the side of mental symptoms, leaving out the joint and arthritic problems I suffered from, which were similar to his own, though not yet so severe, but which had begun forty years earlier). He had to picture me before him as a robust son, *mens sana in corpore sano*, and ignore the fact that, to judge by symptoms, I had long ago, in my late teens, entered a phase of decline which foreclosed many hopes and possibilities early on (while opening others, as I gradually realized) and which in fact resembled his old age in its tactics of sombre parsimony, right down to his practical routines, and their psychological equivalents, of diligently searching out non-perishable foods on sale, buying these in quantity, and stacking and counting the cans and packages in a basement pantry. Still, despite these paradoxes, I frequently left his side feeling rejuvenated, as if I had in fact become the inspiring, vigorous man he needed me to be. It was his own younger self, I think, a tireless and indomitable man untouched by sickness or signs of frailty until his mid-sixties, whom he summoned to stand or sit in my place, and I welcomed this magical transposition almost as much as he did, quickened by an aura of slowly fading energy that lasted sometimes for several hours after our meetings.

No one by the fire was pressuring me to speak. They had all expressed relief that the party was occurring at all, but I felt it incumbent on me to say or do something ceremonial. The fact that everyone was avoiding putting me on the spot made me feel all the more indebted to them and obliged to return some measure of grace for grace. Clearing my throat by way of introduction, I attempted a short speech of thanks, which, owing to my soft and faltering delivery, fell flat, never quite capturing everyone's attention. As I spoke, I was aware of talking in pockets around me, which did not seem like rudeness so much as simple obliviousness of a speaker who was himself half willing to disappear. The depressed speak often in such stale and halting tones that it is like listening to an old, faded tape, down to the soft hissing static that seems to blanket their utterances like a sibilant fog, which, if it is not the subvocal sound of depression itself, may be due to the depressed person's inability to enunciate crisply, each word rising thickly through a swamp of possible sounds and dribbling into the next, creating a miasma that expresses nothing so plainly as its own ignorability. When I stopped, there was an awkward pause, with people breaking their conversations to look around, just as there is when the background tape spools to its end, leaving dead air. I reached into my canvas bag and retrieved the three large chocolate bars and fifty sparklers I had purchased for this moment. After a long period of blankness regarding my birthday—with seemingly no thoughts or feelings about it, other than a vague foreboding about what might rush in to fill such a vacuum—I had had a vision, the day before we left Toronto, of a simple ritual: my parents lighting their sparklers and then touching the scintillating wands to those of their children, who would light up others—a passing of the torch—a chain of glorious shooting fire until the last one was extinguished.

Complications soon arose, however, which gave me a new appreciation for the complexities of event planning. Sparklers are short-lived and require considerable dexterity if one is to light the next one, touching red-hot core to stem, before the first goes out. And if this rapid chaining is to begin with two people nearing eighty, who have had several drinks? And if Sue has added thirty sparklers of her own to the pile, making for an even more ungovernable total of eighty (the number of my parents' years, not mine)? Finally, as if to guarantee that things could not go as planned, I had already passed out the jumbo chocolate bars to the children, who now, their blood rampant with sugar, were jumping about and clamouring for the fun to begin. My planned rite of elegant chaos quickly devolved into a true chaos of wildly sparking wands waving and swirling dangerously close to one another, a melee of hissing arcs of light that made an accident not only probable but inevitable. Later, in the photo Greg e-mailed me, I would see five-year-old Jimmy laughing amid starry white jots, a moment of excited hilarity frozen in digital bits, just before he scorched his finger on the sparkler core and needed prolonged consoling inside the cabin, while he wailed and sobbed and held a face cloth filled with ice to his red and already blistering finger. When I entered the cabin to see if I could help, he stopped his crying for a moment to look up at me with eyes that seemed more bewildered than accusatory. I was the grown-up who had passed out sparklers by the handful and then lit and waved them more frantically than anyone else, filling the night with raucous shooting lights that exhilarated just before they seared. Sue was packing more ice cubes into the face cloth, and I was taken back in time to another, more serious French River debacle, at the only winter festivity we ever attempted there, when Dad and I, one half-frozen and the other petrified, lurched through the back door of the cottage to find Mom holding a wash cloth filled with ice to Greg's copiously bleeding head. Outside, thirty-eight years and two seasons later, Greg suggested wryly that I go into children's party planning. "Chocolate bars for everyone followed by eighty sparklers." He grinned, and we all chuckled quietly. It seemed a jibe aimed less at the childlessness that Heather and I have chosen, and more at the stoical but surprising and resourceful child I had remained, one who would endure a leaden weight of night in silence, then oppose it suddenly with updrafts of uproariousness.

ᘓ   "Where's Greg?" Mom asked, not long before she and Dad left in their boat to go home. By now the differences in their temperaments, made starker by age and tiredness and drink, could be read in their contrasting postures: Dad slumped in disgruntlement; Mom perched stiffly, her eyes flicking about. Perhaps a mother has an anxiety she never loses about the location of her children: Is everyone here? Are they all accounted for? Mom had always been quick to point out examples of this in the animal world: ducks marshalling the stragglers as they swim along a shore (up to a point, past which the straggler must be allowed to straggle, with all the likely fatal risk that implies); a mother bullhead corralling her myriad young, like a dark ewe herding her all-black lambs in a ragged, milling circle that somehow spirals forward. And if at least one of your children has disappeared for long periods into a perilous zone, then the anxiety may become permanent (one of us, Sarah, was absent even now, settling into a new house with her children after the collapse of her marriage).

Before she could ask after him again, Greg walked out of the woods with Ebony. Greg is an outdoorsman, an avid duck hunter and fisherman, and he stepped forward from the opaque trees as naturally as an actor slipping out from between stage curtains. Looking up, I saw a version of myself (Jimmy still mixes up our names), of the same height and similar proportions, but younger (by six and a half years), handsomer, stronger and healthier. Thinking back now to that sight of him, I want to put a gun in his hand—I can feel the narrative actually *leaning* toward this inclusion, as if it were a physical force I must resist, and sometimes the gun actually appears, long and vivid and clear, and the effort to remove it feels like a careful peeling away or erasure—as if this prop of a weapon is needed to complete the otherwise perfect image of the solitary hunter emerging from the woods at night, to render a truth that could exceed or encompass the facts. This was not the first time I had invented, or tried not to invent, an extra bit of business for Greg in a scene from one of the Black River stories I kept trying to write. In the account of our winter trip, I kept wanting to add the fictitious detail of Greg almost drowning playing crack the whip on the partially frozen river. I would become impatient with my own imagination, as if it were a wayward child, and wonder why a true-life story that had enough real blood and freezing and near-death was insisting on this fanciful and superfluous fright.

The party became more boisterous after my parents left and the pace of drinking, never slow in a bibulous family, quickened further. As usual, Chris dominated the talk; three years Greg's senior, the middle child, he is a small-town doctor and bon vivant, who brings imposing energies to bear on any situation. But I have trouble following Chris's jokes and stories even in my most upbeat moods, and now I let them swell and rumble around me, along with the guffaws and rejoinders they provoked, like surf upon a pebbled beach, only smiling occasionally to defer being asked for a more substantial contribution. Thus dispensed, I was free to continue musing upon the figure of the hunter I had seen. Greg collaborated with me in this by regularly getting up and slipping back into the forest for a few minutes, far more regularly than his bladder would have required, as if he had some business there that he had to keep returning to, or as if he needed regular infusions of dark isolation to fuel his vigorous participation in the campfire circle. Hunters of tale and fable strode through my mind. Orion, the autumn giant, not yet visible, under whose glittering auspices I had so often entered my own blackest reaches, voids so remote and frozen that returns from them took creeping time and periods of suspended animation. Staring into the changing flames, as even the most garrulous talkers were doing, I recalled that Orion was slain by Diana (just why, I had forgotten) and that his constellation is supposed to be attended by stormy weather, and further, that he had been blinded (again, I wasn't sure how or why) and that Vulcan had sent him a guide, before his sight was restored by exposing his eyeballs to the sun. In my twenties I had been enthralled by the novels of Knut Hamsun; *Pan* and *Hunger*, in particular, I read over and over. Thomas Glahn, the hero of *Pan*, has "something wrong" with him—the phrase is repeated, insisted upon, by himself and others, until it comes to seem, not frustratingly vague, but rather the most precise formulation available for the protean ecstasies and despairs that whirl him about. Glahn lives in a forest hut (or in the forest itself, where he often chooses to sleep), alone except for his dog Aesop, and only the ancient routines of hunting seem to bring him some stability, some focus for his tumultuous passions. In human company these energies become obsessive, paranoid, ultimately disastrous. His fixation on the girl, Edvarda, which seems as accidental as any other desire in the melee of his soul, is doomed even as it begins. After many fraught, and a few joyous, episodes, Glahn shoots himself on purpose in the foot, shoots his beloved Aesop in the neck, and finally, we learn in an epilogue, is shot dead himself, in a faraway country, by a jealous rival he has deliberately provoked. His curtly brooding self-assessment, "I merely long to go away . . . for I belong to the forests and the solitude," seems, like the "something wrong," to be simultaneously inadequate and the most that can be said about his state. Ernest Hemingway, of course, the arch-hunter himself, also wrote stories about doomed hunters, "The Snows of Kilimanjaro" and "The Short Happy Life of Francis Macomber" being two of the most famous and successful. Like Glahn, Hemingway's hunters are essential solitaries, though in a more secretive and ironic way, since their entanglements with women, with guides and fellow hunters and servants, are being steadily eaten away by some private blot—which may be called gangrene or cowardice—that acts like a powerful acid, with no base to neutralize it, dissolving their ties to society and to life itself. Hemingway's stories do not normally feature a dog, partly because big game hunting does not require one, but more, I think, because Hemingway, like his fictional stand-ins, was both dog and hunter himself, so the drama, the internal division, could not be split between two external beings. One character was black dog and lean hunter, or black hunter and lean dog, both joined and jostling in one man to see which would be ultimate master. And it is not just the knowledge of Hemingway's own end (though this seems, falsely, to cinch the matter) that creates the aura of potential suicide that seems to hover over stories of hunters, especially solitary ones. Such stories inculcate an atmosphere of lurking, vaguely directed menace that can make them seem like stories of suicide deferred. It is a part of the palpable suspense such stories easily generate, along with the naturally propulsive action of the chase. The sombre single-mindedness of the hunt itself, the stalking and tracking and meditating upon spoors, and the solitude of isolated men—the Macombers, the Glahns—can add up to an impression of temporizing, using a provisional quarry, until the weapon can swivel round to find its true target. And all of the musings upon the ethics and methods of the hunt, which carry so much more weight than the actual hunt seems able to bear, always read like musings upon the grounds of life itself and upon one's bearing in it and of it.

It was during these musings of my own, solitary broodings by which I hunted for something in the midst of my own celebration, that a fox came up and stood at the rim of the circle of light shed by our fire. It stood motionless, seemingly unafraid, the light from the flames around the logs we had piled high rippling over its reddish fur, picking out the snow whiteness of its eyes in the glare. The first person to spot it exclaimed in surprise, and the rest of us followed suit. We all agreed—the fox just standing there as we discussed it—that our occasional sightings of this animal had always been at a distance or on the run, a flash of russet on the road ahead or a tawny-white slinking over a hillside. Greg, though, the better naturalist, explained that foxes, like most carnivores, are opportunistic and will frequent human habitations more tamely if food can be obtained safely there. Cabins rented to tourists, who cook meat over open fires and are often careless about leftovers and garbage, offer ideal conditions for such scavenging. Where's Eb? I thought suddenly as Greg was explaining this, realizing that there could not be a large dog anywhere nearby and that the fox must have known this. It stood unperturbed, its sharp face still and its fur luminous; it did not move a hair as Greg got out his digital camera and snapped its picture, and the image he later e-mailed might well have been that of a stuffed fox under a blaze of photographer's lights, overexposed for a deliberate effect, except for the unfeignable fierceness, a tense alertness in the slightly cocked face, in the eyes especially. Soon the fox walked unhurriedly around the far rim of the camp circle and disappeared into the woods on the other side. A few minutes later, Greg took one of his walks into the woods near where the fox had vanished. This kept happening over the next couple of hours: the curious fox appearing and then leaving, Greg leaving and returning, sometimes one first and then the other, from different directions around our semicircle of chairs, as if hunter and quarry were circling in slow motion in a perpetual chase through our midst. Watching these seemingly coordinated movements, which no one else noticed or at any rate commented on, and raising my eyes frequently from our fire to stare at the stars twinkling above our clearing, I lost the sense of a merely earthbound pursuit and imagined the chase, or dance as it more nearly seemed, going on through the star-fields and the vast black voids between them, only intersecting our gathering periodically, as the sun travels among the constellations along the line of its ecliptic.

The natural end to all these hunter thoughts, their culmination so to speak, was Bruegel's great painting *Hunters in the Snow*, which rose so clearly to my mind's eye I might have been standing before it in a gallery. *Hunters in the Snow* was painted by the Flemish master in 1565, four centuries, minus a year or two, before Dad and I walked across the ice of Dry Pine Bay one winter afternoon to find the help we needed. The returning hunters are on a rise above the snowbound village. A pack of lean hounds follow their masters.

The townspeople and their pastimes are far below, distant. Tiny figures skating, wielding curved sticks or brooms to play a version of hockey or curling, on the small rectangles of grayish ice, like clouded mirrors, they have claimed, scraped free from their shrouds of snow. The eye reverts warily to the three hunters in the foreground left. Close to the viewer, they are large, of course, twice as large as some figures outside a nearby inn, six or seven times as large as the insect people at their frozen games below; yet in all the vast human panorama, only one man, washing a round table by a fire outside the inn, has turned his head to register their approach. We see the backs of the hunters, not their faces. They are dark, dark as the bare trees they move among (the top half of the lead man merges with some foliage, only the inverted V of his striding legs silhouetted against the snow), their caps and leggings black as the crows perched in the leafless branches or the crow that has launched itself to glide on ragged wings above the unsuspecting villagers. Thin and thinly dressed, no doubt cold and tired, the hunters do not stop to warm themselves by the sociable fire outside the inn. Plodding through deep snow, they seem more than stoical and resolute, they seem implacable, striking down the steep slope in arrowhead formation, descending upon a populace they might, by their attitudes and equipage, as well mean to slaughter as to provision.

Not wanting to leave too early, but lacking the energy to stay very late (the party would go on till 4:00 a.m., we later learned), Heather and I settled for an awkward compromise, departing just a few minutes before the official start of my birthday at midnight, though it felt hours later to me, as if at the very limit of an interminable night that must be nearing dawn. Greg helped us down a brushy, root-knotted slope and across slippery planks laid across the mud to reach the rickety dock, just as two hours earlier he and I had helped my parents down and across the same tricky route. Bats and nighthawks veered in black smears overhead, chasing the mosquitoes we had drawn out with us. After we had untied and had paddled a little out into the shallow, weedy bay, there came a sudden loud squawk, or quack, from a bird we had startled, probably a duck or loon, followed by splashy flapping until it found the air. The sound was one certain, I thought, to turn Greg's head, but when I looked back I could barely make him out on the planks below the slope, striding back into the woods as he had been doing all night long. Off to his right was the fire in the clearing, the contrast between the orange leaping flames and the black forest too extreme to make out the people seated somewhere between them. But their voices carried to us faintly, fragments of talk and laughter. I paddled us a little farther out, enjoying the silent bay with its sweetly skunky smell of weeds, out to where I knew the water was already quite deep, not far, perhaps a hundred yards to the east, from where one of the Black River events I had so often tried, and just as often failed, to write had occurred.

Ᏻ I must have tried a dozen versions of the story of the woman who drowned herself. A dozen different stories, not counting the many drafts of each of those. Maybe a hundred stories—a thousand pages, say—of that one story. They all came out flat, stillborn. Or else with fatal defects, unintended complexities that twisted their limbs and faculties so they could not operate as they should. A common problem was that a relatively simple storyline would be strangled by the coils of all that it was being made to say, by the umbilical cord that connected it to real life and events, to the parent that had conceived it and nourished it so far but which now

entangled and overwhelmed it. In all those trials it never occurred to me to first set down what I actually remembered.

We were having breakfast at the long pine table that
looked west across Dry Pine Bay. It must have been August,
because that was when Dad took his holidays. In July it was
just Mom and the five of us. After breakfast, I was taking Sue
and Greg fishing in one of the back lakes we often portaged
into. It was rare that Dad, with his lifelong passion for fishing, would not be leading such a trip, and I can't remember
why he was staying behind this time. I would have been fourteen or fifteen, Sue two years younger, Greg four and a half
years younger still. As we finished up, Mom was watching
the far shore through binoculars, something she often
did—she enjoyed especially the bustle of boats leaving the
Lift-the-Latch Lodge dock—but today she kept lifting the
black lenses from her eyes and settling them again. "That's
odd," she said a couple of times. Or, "Strange." Something
like that.

It emerged—at first just as pregnant, vaguely omi-
nous looks between my parents, then afterward, piecemeal,
as the beginning of a story whose end I had participated
in—that Mrs. V., a long-time cottager across the river, was
preparing to drown herself. Of course, that was not what
Mom and Dad said, or perhaps even guessed, at the time.
What they said, as they exchanged the binoculars, in answer
to our pestering questions, was that Mrs. V. was behaving
oddly as she went for an early morning dip, walking into the
water then out again, then in again, splashing her face with
water, all with her housecoat on. Her housecoat was the
splotch of rosebud pink we could make out just above the
water, seeming, without the binoculars, to float on it like a
pink lotus. It all sounded odd, but Mrs. V. had done other
odd things. She was a known drunk, in her sixties, who, since

her doctor husband had become involved with another woman, was now left alone at the cottage they had shared with their children in happier years. A pathetic story, but a familiar one. I would not have felt so uneasy, as if something terrible was gathering that could not be discussed—except for those looks between my parents. They were what made me ask if I should stay or go as planned.

Whenever I watch hospital dramas, with people in masks trading freighted looks, I think of my parents, for whom such charged glances must be intensely nostalgic, taking them back to their time of courtship. Mom had been the head nurse, and Dad the new intern, on the ward when they met. "My boss," he jokes, and they share a smile at both the joke and at its complex, unspoken coda, which might be *For the first and last time* . . . . For fifty-five years they have shared that intricate drama of the eyes, in which work shading into romance, the potential and the actuality of a life lived together, must all be blended indissolubly.

Go, go on, Dad told me, in a rough tone that would brook no resistance. Later I would wonder at this haste to send us off on our fishing trip. If we had left two minutes sooner, we would not have seen what we saw. But as well, there would have been no boat left for anyone to cross the river with, and we had no telephone. Dad, as I sensed then and saw more clearly later, has had a complex relationship with crisis, a balance in constant need of adjustment, in terms of thought and action, between the wish to let catastrophe occur unhindered and, if possible, unseen, and the Hippocratic oath and medical skills that bind and equip him to avert at least some kinds of disaster. Only in his career of surgery, of all possible medical fields, could he find, I think, the fulcrum by which a team led by him could try, for a specified period, by agreed-on means, to shift a weight of pain and disease, but also by virtue of which the team could sur-render honourably if, in spite of everything, the load proved too great. Efforts could be superb, even heroic, without needing to be unlimited. That sounds curiously like the dis-tinction often made between the role of a father and a mother.

The story of Mrs. V.'s drowning dissolves into frag-ments if I tell it without invention, as I would like to finally. Just luminous bits, moments that gleam with the milky hard-ness of pearls, moments that have survived all the subse-quent ravagings of memory, like jewels hoarded through a war—a necklace of an event, which needs some ordinary thread to hold its parts together in a fixed sequence, a nor-mally invisible string, which I must rely on but cannot trust, to line these things up so that they can happen on one sum-mer morning. Dad striding quickly down the ramp to the dock, saying to me, We've got to go across. He and I heaving the canoe off of the gunwales back onto the dock. (Greg and Sue must already have been sitting in the boat, but that is thread, not memory. They had to have been there so I could see their faces later, on the other side.) We speed across the blue water, silver spray in sunlight. Dad is pointing but I know the bay. As we near the place, he rises to a crouch and points more forcefully, jabbing his finger at a spot in the wa-ter. I slow down, half standing now too, though I can see nothing yet. Hurry, don't slow, he tells me, with a look and windmill gestures. But I am afraid of chewing her up in the propellor. Then I see: a pink cloud in the water amidst the weeds, with a gray fuzzy spot in the middle of it—her head, just under the surface. Now he is slapping the air downward as if spanking it, Slow down, Slow down—I can't get my speed right—and we come alongside too fast and both of us must lunge to grab a piece of her. An arm, a fistful of drenched pink. A dead weight—I feel in my arms and back what this means in terms of a person. But Dad is a strong man, and I am coming into my strength, and we hoist her over the side, her lolling head clunking against the side and bottom of the boat. Everything about her is sodden, mushy-looking: her drenched gray hair, white slack face leaking water and some thicker liquid, the sopping pink housecoat rucked up around her waist, her flabby thighs and skinny legs whitest and softest of all. (This is when I see, a flashbulb glimpse, my brother and sister staring with wide eyes from the front seat.) Dad jabs his finger at the point nearby, meaning Lift-the-Latch's dock on the other side of it, and then we are veering in a tight arc, gunwale close to the water so that Dad must pin her body to prevent her falling out again, and heading straight for the busy dock. Tourists, guides, the owner, milling—no boats have left yet, there is no open space. I aim for a sliver of dock between a bow and a motor, slow down, then speed up, and again strike too fast, with a heavy clunk. Arms haul her out and flop her down—another clunk—on the green-painted dock. Bodies press forward, talking excitedly, and voices tell them to step back, to give room. She's drown-ded for sure, says a man I know, a long-time guide from the village. (A quarter century later—a future thread that twines with this one—he too will drown, after getting drunk in his boat and being carried by the current over Recollet Falls.) Dad, who is already thumping her chest, motions this man to begin mouth-to-mouth resuscitation. The man looks aghast, but goes to one knee to try. After one or two shallow passes at her mouth, he rears back with a blanched, stricken expression. He stumbles to his feet mumbling, I can't, I can't, Doc. I kneel in his place. Pinch nose, cup chin, arch neck. Slack skin, limp and flabby. Water, slime. Seal her mouth, breathe out, turn, breathe in. A sickly, sweet-musty smell in my nostrils—perfume and weeds, algae, it smells like (mixed with alcohol, I will be told later). The thumps of Dad's heart massage are hard, harder than I would have imagined such a procedure could be. Each time I turn my head, as I learned to do in some First Aid class, I see his joined hands pound her chest, and I feel the shuddering force of the blows travel through her inert body into me. Finally, after he has stopped but I have not, he says to me, She's gone, Mike. I think he had to say it more than once, in different words, before I stopped. She's dead. That's it. She's gone.

After that, my memory of the morning is fuzzier, more narrative threads than sensory pearls (the latter, it occurs to me now, I called "loss luminous, horror pearls" in a poem about another acutely disturbing event). I remember standing slump-shouldered back at our own dock, feeling sick at heart but also keyed up, unreal. Partly this would have been a normal chemical reaction, the adrenaline that had powered me through the crisis now decaying into adrenochrome and other murky by-products. I had no interest in going on with the fishing trip as planned, but Dad told me that I had to go—or that it was important we go . . . I can't remember his exact words. I don't remember him saying why it was important, if he knew himself. I remember bridling inwardly, though I would have given no outward sign, not at the idea that life must go on, but at the insistence that it go on so promptly, without a decent pause. The sorrow and aversion I have felt all my adult life at the human zeal to rush past events—and my shame at my own skill in doing so—as if the significant moments of our lives are faces on a platform and we the riders on a train that does not make unscheduled stops—acquired new intensity, if it did not actually begin, on this morning in August.

We tied the canoe back across the middle of the boat and set off upriver. French River flows roughly east to west, and the ride upriver in the morning is especially dazzling, with the water sparkling under the climbing sun, the trees and lichened rocks freshened by drying dew. The beauty filled my eyes as much, or more, than ever; I was young and strong and capable, and I opened my nostrils wide to take in fragrant air—but at the same time, my contentment kept catching at itself, dividing like an amoeba into mirror factions: one part supremely conscious of being alive, joyous and grateful to be so; the other half wondering what it would be like not to be. I asked the questions that have not changed since long before Hamlet voiced them, the same questions anyone would ask, in the same ways; staring across the chasm between everything and nothing, revolving the ancient and unanswerable mystery in my mind. I can feel this wind on my face, in my hair. She cannot. I smell pines and cedar, hear water sluicing, brace my thighs against the surge of waves—she does none of these. An hour ago she had memories, thoughts, wishes . . . now, none?

By the time we got to Shield's Lake, about an hour's trip, my thoughts had settled into this morbid groove. To Sue and Greg—who, as far as I can remember, maintained a near perfect silence about what had happened—I played my part of the capable and cheerful older brother, chatting from the stern of the canoe as I paddled us around the shore, directing their casts, netting their fish, baiting their hooks. All the while spinning in the same eddy of questions, which was only one question differently phrased: I am here, in Shield's Lake . . . where is she? I am unhooking a bass; she is—? Where her body had been, at least, I would learn later that day. Someone had got a tarpaulin from the boathouse and laid it over her, and she had lain under it on the dock for two or three hours, until the police had driven up the highway from Britt and taken the required statements. Now, in the depressed aftermath, I remembered the fright and excitement of crisis with something like nostalgia. Contrary to what newscasters and other adult moralizers maintain, emergencies are seldom times of confusion and dithering, and almost never the hardest tests of character. Those features are more true of the periods before and after crisis, or when a crisis prolongs itself and becomes a siege, wearing down the nerves and threatening to crumble resistance. Acute crisis itself, however, can actually lift you free of time into a dispensed, even a serene, zone in which the actions that are indisputably required can be easily identified and, by most people, accomplished. I had behaved well in a crisis, done the necessary under pressure—not like the man who quit and stumbled back.

It strikes me as odd now—though I can't recall ever thinking of it before this moment—that in all the times, beginning within two years after that day, that I myself stood at the brink of self-destruction—blade in hand, girder or ledge under my feet—it was never the multiple indignities and sordidness of Mrs. V.'s death, nor even its baffling finality, that pulled me back from slash or leap, but rather the seething complexity, which by then was life itself, ravelled up in my parents' shared glances beforehand and my own seething melancholy afterward. That complexity was what I longed to escape, but could never quite relinquish. That was what I wished to cancel, to un-know, but it was all I knew. It was also what I craved to know better, to one day get to the bottom of, even, in my wildest, greediest dreams, to comprehend fully. Not to annul, but to apprehend utterly. Already, so soon after Mrs. V.'s death, while her body still lay steaming under an oil- and fish-stained canvas, her actual mortal end was being distilled into an essence that permeated my sense of myself and the world, seeping away from the surface of consciousness and percolating, through fissures and hair-line cracks, down to nourish the roots of dread and dreadful longing. My senses all felt heightened, especially the sense of smell. No other sense retrieves a time so commandingly, and to this day the sweetish, weedy stink that encircles lakes and hovers over swamps still takes me back immediately to that August morning. All that day, and for many days afterward, I smelled that sweet-rot essence, the perfume-and-bog mix-ture that was unforgettable and yet ineffable: in the air; on my hands, which I kept washing; in my nose and mouth, where I knew I could not get rid of it. At times, things came to my eyes in lurid zooms, as if slid suddenly under a magnify-ing lens. Objects under my fingertips felt terribly hard, crisped or mineralized, then gooey-soft—they felt different, in texture, in shape, in every way. Yet for all this heightening of my senses, I myself, sitting inside them so to speak, like the hollow at the core of a stack of vividly painted dolls, felt dreamy, dream-like—disconnected, as if experience had es-tranged me from the world by plunging me too forcefully into one pungent part of it.

I kept seeing weeds. We cast our frogs at the weeds, at lily pads like the ones the frogs had basked on before we trapped them in our filthy pail. We pulled leaping bass out from under the swaying stalks, and snapping turtles paddled out after the bass we had caught, murky shapes hovering like brown, beaked shoals in the weeds around the canoe, just out of range of a paddle swat. The weeds were everywhere I looked. Thick slimy tubes that encompassed three elements: rooted in muck, climbing through water, massing at the sur-face, poking at air. But the weeds I saw went beyond these el-ements. The grass under water climbed up beaches and became grass on land, as if those tall green plants just kept going, unstoppable. They were like the terra cotta soldiers in the Chinese emperor's tomb in *Life*, excavated on an incline, and still only partially, so that some stood fully exposed in light, some were still half buried in dirt, and some you knew were unseen and far below, completely covered in the dark. Turn to face the other way and you would see these weed regiments continue marching up an incline to infinity, all the way until their inconceivably giant forms stood guard in the blackness of space, heads swaying among the stars.

ରଃ Stars, in fact, their glittering panorama overhead, were what I raised my eyes to view as we skimmed over the calm black water back up Dry Pine Bay toward our room. The middle of the bay was deep at this end, but I travelled at half speed to prolong the journey, which I was enjoying more than anything I had all night, and then I slowed even further. Heather, who is not a confident swimmer, darted a look back at me, as if I might have spotted an unlit boat or other danger on the water, but when I smiled and pointed up, she settled more comfortably in her seat, switching off our flashlight. I thought of stopping the motor to view the stars while floating on the quiet river—at last, I thought, that might finish one year properly and usher in the next—but I resisted the urge. All my impulses to sacralize moments had thus far failed, most notably the after-dinner speech that I had struggled to get out and that had gone mostly unheard, and the only truly meaningful moments of the evening had been accidental. It is partly this—my greater faith in hazard and digression than in planned unfoldings—that has led people to call me flexible and agreeable, qualities which are true enough but only partly for the reasons they think. I seldom believe in the main plan, the stated one; even less often do I believe that it is what it says it is. So there is little to be lost by deviations, some of which may throw up magic that the mainline buried. Now, for instance, the drone of our motor made a trance-like sound, blocking outside awareness. Turn it off and snatches of conversation, calls for dogs, bits of music and tinklings of ice would follow us out here; we would drift as passive guests around the rims of many parties. So we kept going, and looked up at the stars. I counted the ones I knew in my head, not as many as before we moved to the city ten years ago. Cassiopeia, off to the right. The Big Dipper, with its pointer stars leading to Polaris. Draco rearing up between them. The Summer Triangle, right overhead: Deneb in Cygnus, Vega in Lyra, and further "down" and behind us, so that I had to turn in my seat and look south toward the fire circle we had left, Altair in Aquila. Each of the stars of the Summer Triangle had its own story, but a story could be told—or pieces of a story, pregnant suggestions—between them, too. A story stretching across light-years of black void, a story of the sun and prideful error leading to watery death, but leading past this, finally, to sky and earthly humility, the service given by boy to god, which must begin in force, in rapture, but may end in devotion and even love. The contours of this larger story gleam out when you handle the individual stories familiarly, even a bit carelessly, letting their polished wholes fall away and shatter, and then wander among the shards, picking and wondering at these contributory parts, sensing a larger artifact that can be at least partially reassembled. You have to get a bit drunk on the stories; you have to reel and ramble among them. Phaethon, reckless son of the early sun god, Helios, is an Icarus figure, flying in an ecstasy of power too high for his young gifts, except that the danger he poses is not only to himself but to the world, which he threatens to set on fire through his recklessness. Killed pre-emptively by

Zeus, he falls from his sun chariot into the river Eridanus. His sky-blazing hubris and watery nemesis prefigure the later, more human-scaled and pathetic, fall of Icarus, curtly dropped by Bruegel (who wants back into this essay and won't be kept out much longer) and picked up, picked out, by W. H. Auden. In some variants of the Phaethon story there is a poignant coda in which his friend (or brother) Cygnus dives in after him, dies himself, and for this abortive rescue or devoted suicide is turned into the heavenly swan in which Deneb burns. Vega, light-years away but a hand's span to my eyes, shines in Lyra, the lyre of Orpheus. Phaethon, the too-tasked juvenile, was "too much in the sun." Orpheus, though, a later figure, will display a mature mastery in daylight, when the sun has become more than burning globe and is associated with the light and reason of Apollo, who gives Orpheus his lyre. Armed with his art, Orpheus performs well on water too—as one of Jason's Argonauts he helps to conquer the Clashing Rocks and the Sirens with his music—but in another sense, the master musician has, like Ophelia, "too much of water," or else not enough. Love binds him to Eurydice, who, as a nymph or dryad, is a creature from the woods, a being at home in dewy haunts of leaves and pools and trickling streams. But something— some insufficiency in Orpheus, the myth always implies— stands in the way of this union, prevents it from being enduring or perhaps even consummated. Trying to bring Eurydice back from the underworld, he looks back at the last moment and loses her; later, a miserable wanderer, he is torn to pieces by maenads and reduced to a pathetic severed head (wanly rendered by Odilon Redon), singing as it floats down a river. In either phase of the torments of Orpheus, the loss of Eurydice or the carnage of his end, there is implied the same weakness, an insufficiency at the core, an effete mastery that is already somehow bodiless. In his supreme obedience to the rule of Apollo does he neglect the equally stringent rites of Dionysus, drowning in light for lack of the dark? Orpheus has evolved far beyond the hubristic joy ride of Phaethon, who might almost be his far younger brother, but still something is lacking in him when he attempts to journey deeper into the sources of mystery (the underworld, the woods) and he suffers a like ruin for his incompleteness. Neither Phaethon nor Orpheus is a suicide in the strict sense, but both are on suicidal paths; higher powers recognize this and end their lives. Myth, though, in its hardness, gives no assurances of the attainability of a completeness that could have saved Orpheus from his fate. His art grants him power over the world's secret magic but also separates him from the deepest participation in it; the story is a witheringly accurate view of the artist in terms of both his powers and their limitations. For fleeting mastery he pays the ultimate price, but no myth will ever whisper that there is another price, or a better deal to be struck.

Turning to find the last point of the Summer Triangle meant turning in the north-running boat to face the south and the receding dot of yellow fire in the clearing where my family did its touching best to mark my fiftieth year and succeeded to the extent my depressed spirits would allow. The last star, Altair, is in Aquila, which is shaped like a kite or a bird with wings outstretched. The constellation pricks out its white dotted outline against black, in exact tonal contrast to the black bird of Bruegel (who will not stay out of this much longer), spreading solid wings above pale snow. Aquila was an eagle that belonged to Zeus (or was Zeus, since he took his human lovers in various guises including that of a swan), which carried Ganymede, a Trojan prince that Zeus desired, up into the heavens to serve as Zeus's cup bearer. Though the myth has been variously allegorized as homosexual love, ideal or Platonic love, or even the victory of patriarchy over matriarchy as represented by Cybele and other mother goddesses, for my purposes on this night I squint at it along another tangent entirely. Phaethon and Orpheus were upward-strivers, subject to immediate or eventual rebuff by the gods. Ganymede's flight to the stars was involuntary, however; he was snatched and soared. Rembrandt's picture of him as a chubby infant wailing and struggling in implacable talons, captures, if not the extension of Zeus's boundless lust into pedophilia, then another hard assertion by myth: that it may not be our competent and assured adult selves, with all their determined flappings upward, but rather ourselves at our most naked and vulnerable and unwilling and even undeserving, that mighty forces seize on to snatch and pluck clear of gravity.

That is just one cluster of meaning that could be picked from this storied chaos. The uncertainty, their ragged edges and shifting elements, are just what I love most about the old myths. They have such a fluid, plastic sense about them, whether by design or because in their transmission different tellers have altered or emphasized different details. The tales themselves admit this frequently: *In some versions of the story* . . . . They are permissive tapestries: they will allow you—an allowance that can be abused, of course—to locate a stray thread and tug on it a little, crinkling the overall design. Or, indeed, you can stare at just the one loose thread, if that is all you can take in at the time. Sometime in October, a couple of months after my birthday party, when on a new regimen of pills I was starting to feel a bit better, Heather and I visited my parents at their home in Burlington. Sue and Jimmy were the other guests for dinner. Dad, who daily grows more subject to bouts of nostalgia that bring him to the point of tears (his eyes fill up so suddenly, without his seeming to be aware of it, it is as if the past itself, the weight of it, is literally squeezing water out of him), was talking about his experiences as a sailor in World War II. During these reminiscences I glanced at Jimmy, who is often quickly bored by adult talk. But he was standing for the moment quietly beside me, watching and listening to his grandfather. Already he seemed much older than the child of two months before, with new powers of concentration. He sits down in a low chair, hands on knees, as if to listen better. What could these stories of ships and U-boats mean to him? I wondered. Or The War (for he would hear unmistakably the majuscules in our voices)? For Dad, actual memories, which became for me in childhood oft-repeated stories, corroborated and enlarged by other people's stories and by books and movies and factual evidence of every kind, converge in a web of truth so extensive that it leaves no room for doubt. If an adult were to deny that World War II occurred, we would take that denial as evidence of mental derangement. Yet to five-year-old Jimmy, born fifty-five years after that war ended, the knowledge that such an event occurred may rest, to begin with, on the mere assertion of it by a teacher, parent, or book. Which joins to many such assertions, by many different sorts of people. What he feels about this story-spinning war is not a fact or certainty in the undeniable sense that he feels his body sitting in a chair, but it must impress him with a heaviness, a gravity, that is memorable long after the temporary push of his flesh against wooden supports has been forgotten. What he feels is the (ultimately very real) weight of absolute belief, of conviction. He follows Dad downstairs, and they come back with a cigar box of navy memorabilia. Jimmy passes round Dad's induction photo—"That's Grandpa"—pointing to the seventeen-year-old face that only very vaguely resembles the one he knows. Dad gives him his HMCS Ottawa crest to keep, the first item from this box I have seen him give away. Jimmy, still absorbed and attentive, gripped by something, passes round more black and white photos, reminded by Sue and then reminding others to handle them by their edges. "This was Grandpa's boat. It got hit by another boat." To my comment, "Yes, I see the hole in the bow," he returns a fervent shaking of the head. "It didn't sink," he declares. "Grandpa's boat didn't sink."

And now, suddenly—as if memory itself were a skimmer on water, or a walker on ice, who can break through at any moment and plunge to forgotten depths—I remember more about Orion. He was already a giant, a rather bizarre watery one, long before his stellar transfiguration. A son of Poseidon, he was so huge that he strode through oceans with his head above them, though that is not where he operated as a hunter (not a swallower of schools of fish or a wrestler of whales). He hunted on land, and with such supreme savagery that he denuded one island of all its animals. As an extension of this ultimate hunt, or the object of it, he raped a woman, Merope, for which he was blinded by her father. (That is a strange feature of giants in all stories, the way their scale shifts to suit the story, to make it possible. So big he can wade the Mediterranean, yet small enough that a mortal woman can suffer his lust and her outraged father can maim him. Then huge again when he is required to be—the story seeing him through one end of the telescope then the other.) Vulcan, out of pity, gave him a guide, Kedalion, and with this helper on his shoulders, Orion wandered the seas in search of the sun god, who would restore his sight by exposing his eyeballs to the sun. In all versions he meets his end at the hand of Artemis—who might have wished his death as a rival hunter, as a protector of the land, as a moon deity, or simply as a woman—but in one version Apollo has an inadvertent hand in Orion's demise. Orion was wading far out in deep water, just like one of the giant weed warriors in my vision, and Apollo, pointing to the black spot that was Orion's head, as disconnected from any apparent body as that of Orpheus, challenged his sister to hit it with one of her arrows. She could, of course, and did.

 C೩ Bruegel. I'm back to him again. Bruegel the sentimental favourite, the genre painter so useful to calendar makers as a colourful chronicler of village life: *Peasant Dance, Wedding Dance, Children's Games, The Wedding Banquet, The Harvesters.* (Though *The Beggars,* gaping above their stumps and crutches, would not be suitable even for a winter month.) Those who appreciate Bruegel's harder and more penetrating eye may prefer his readings of iconic scenes, both pagan and Christian: *The Parable of the Sower, The Parable of the Blind, The Fall of Icarus, The Suicide of Saul, The Procession to Calvary, The Numbering at Bethlehem.* But there is still so much more, and even darker, in Bruegel than these. And not just in his Bosch-like *The Fall of the Rebel Angels, The Triumph of Death,* or *Dulle Griet,* in which an apocalyptic female giant, helmeted and armor-clad, strides with a gape of mindless violence, with a raised sword and a basket of trophies, through the carnage and devastation that is her natural terroir. Beyond these, even, lie Bruegel's quietest and darkest observations, canvases that murmur of the portion of darkness that suffuses our everyday lives, a blackness that must be faced squarely since it cannot be lit or safely ignored. *The Dark Day. Hunters in the Snow.* I keep coming back to it.

Moving past the lights on either side of us, chugging in a tranced drone down the centre of the bay toward a cabin, rented and unlit and as yet invisible at the far end of it—travelling thus, done for now with stargazing and just sighting into the darkness ahead of the boat, I had a dizzy sense of repeating the motion of the hunters in the Bruegel painting. Those dark figures move past the fire at the inn without a glance at it, striding wearily but inexorably toward a home or rendezvous in the village, or, more likely, toward a rest and snack, a bit of snatched fuel before they continue their journey up among the snowy crags that rise on the other side of the valley. They mean business, which means movement; they cannot, will not, stop for long. In the same manner I was moving past the lights of settlement, the glowing invitations of a provisional summer, and had moved, in an emotional sense, with sluggish stops of sorrow and remorse, past the fire my family had lit for me in a clearing, because—the full reasons will always be obscure to me, but in a shorthand phrase, because I felt myself to be a hunter in the snow, I was driven on, I could not stop and take my comfort there. Bruegel's painting tells it all in shapes and colours. The down-the-slope, roughly isosceles triangle the three hunters make—a miniature of the Summer Triangle overhead— finds echoes in the many other triangles that punctuate the village below and the frozen land beyond it: crotches of trees, peaks of houses, spires of churches, crags of rock. Snow-covered, or black where the snow cannot stick, these triangles look like facets of a crystal seen in shadow and light, a crystal that has seeded in the saturated solution of the village and whose aspects of frozen motion—funnelling or striking down, thrusting or spiring up—will always be starker and more concentrated than the knobs and knots and bustling vectors the village traces upon its planes. The five figures grouped around the fire outside the inn form a sort of triangle too, but it is a triangle with crucially curving sides

and a rounded, softened tip, making the cosier shape of a parabola. The chartreuse glow of another, more distant village,
and the snaky twinings of a few yellowish vines above the
snow in the foreground form the base of yet another large
compositional triangle that leads the eye back, counter to
the movement of the hunters, to the leaping yellow flames
outside the inn at the picture's left. Bruegel must have
wanted the viewer, so intent on tracking the advancing
hunters, to glance up and back occasionally at the grouping
they had passed by. Above the fire, from a pole in the inn's
roof, hangs a sign with a kneeling, golden-haloed saint—but
the wooden board hangs crookedly, off its hook on one side.
There is a man with a bucket near the fire, washing a four-
legged round table he has tilted towards him; he is the one
who has glanced up to see the hunters going past. A woman
is stirring the fire with a long stick, or perhaps heating an
iron bar. One man is feeding into the fire a bundle of sticks,
the ends already ablaze with orange light. A white-kerchiefed
woman is bringing out another bundle of fuel from inside the
inn; she has just stepped from the doorway and is hidden
from the shoulders down by smoke. More fuel bundles are
piled against the tree. A small child—a girl, it seems, from
her white apron—stands at the rounded tip of the parabola
with her back to us and to the hunters, watching the fire
with bowed head, in an attitude of silent absorption.
Bruegel's brush describes the different colours of flame—reddish at the fire's base, rising in sheets of yellow and platinum,
orange where it catches new fuel—and it captures the time-
less roles and attitudes of people around the hearth or fire
pit, repeated in our own campfire circle earlier: the fuel gath-
erer, the stoker, the watcher, the tender, the worker to the
side. This is the given, immemorial story. But the hunters
move right past it in their hunt for prey, their hunt for other

meaning. They move out of the unknown—the wild—and toward the unknown. One might have said toward the known, the village, but that is not where these hunters tend, not ultimately. The consolations of a homecoming, however meagre, are foreclosed to them; they may have come from the village but now, anarchic, they may not be taken back into it. Such hunters as these have no home to return to: their home is the hunt. All this is brought out clearly by the bypassed communal fire. The hunters have moved past this obvious stopping point, its promise of at least physical warmth, and are pointed like a dark spear tip toward the chilly and populous scene of gray below them, the town without a sign of fire except for the pockets of individual warmth generated by its myriad figures moving over the ice. Some might see the hunters in a shivery interzone between two knowns, the civilized life of community that lies both behind and ahead of them. But the world ahead of them, though filled with people busily having fun (to keep warm?), looks cold and bleak. So to say that they are moving from deeper woods past the inn toward the village does not resolve the paradox these hunters seem to embody. Could it be that they are in a temporal middle ground? A phase of time between the chase in the forest and the return to village life? They are transition figures as well as hunters, and that contributes to their sinister aspect, the menace Bruegel has brought out in their dark clothing, their slouching walk, their dogs and weapons, their spearhead formation as they descend toward the village below. For what stops—and for how long can it stop—a hunter from finding new prey closer at hand, or from being so changed from his time in the forest that he moves past the village as swiftly and regardlessly as he moved past the fire at the inn? One of the clearest and least ambiguous effects of the mental illness that has dogged me for these thirty years and more—or else a tendency already present in my nature but set and hardened by those traumas—is a need for ceaseless motion, or perhaps more accurately, a sensation of always being in movement, in transition, unable to find rest or to feel at rest. It is this above all that allies me with these hunters, who, though they may be freezing, will not stop by the fire; who, if they stop to gnaw meat, do so reluctantly and briefly, as fuel for their next foray.

CR   In May of 1979, the water level of French River reached its highest point in living memory. On a vertical rock just east of Dry Pine Bay, someone chalked and dated a line marking the water's furthest climb. Just as someone doubtless will note—on paper this time, for a rock would be submerged —the record low water mark attained in the summer of 2005. In 1979, I came north with my parents to open the cottage; I remember loading the boat as it floated beside the gas pumps at the marina, three or more feet above the usual docks even at high water. I remember little else about that springtime trip; probably there was little of me left to re-member with. I had only recently been discharged from a psychiatric ward after a year-and-a-half siege. It was really a siege of seven years, beginning with my first serious depres-sion and psychiatric treatment at age seventeen, which cut short my last year of high school and inaugurated a long, chaotic slide away from active and communal life, culminat-ing in the self-mutilation that earned me a diagnosis of schizophrenia and embarked me on the hospitalized ordeal of neuroleptic drugs, electroshock treatments and hy-dra-headed symptoms that came close to killing me, and, in the sense of obliterating all vestiges of my former life, in a way did kill me. My amnesia of that springtime trip north with my parents seems fitting; I could not have accompa-

nied them except as a dazed and depleted survivor, a conva-
lescent with tremors and scars and a battered brain, a
broken and wide-eyed child though nominally a man of
twenty-four, gaping at the debris left by the flood. I must
have seen it as a brief reprieve. I could not guess then that
soon this shivering castaway, a Crusoe from the ward, would
exult in new, or new-found, powers. He would begin again
the practice, burgeoning to obsession, of scribbling in journals, which had consumed the months before hospitalization and had only been slammed shut by the phenothiazines.
He would find a title for the slim, transcendent volume he
envisioned: *Poems Written Between Hospitalizations*. More
than self-consciously wry, a species of gallows humor known
to survivors of the drop, it was a practical working method
for the only future he could envision for himself. A career in
fits and starts, like the course of a comet as seen by earthbound eyes: disappearing for long periods into the icy blackness of a back ward, then zooming into incandescent
close-up. Though this seemed grimly realistic at the time, it
was still a romanticized view, as views from the perspective
of youth always are; even—or especially—views of illness.
Its focus on the poles of blackness and white light ignored,
because they could not be guessed at, the grim gray rigors of
coping that would comprise most of the space-thing's orbit.
Survival wiles: drug trials, rising intakes of sedatives and alcohol, strategic hibernations and withdrawals, dietary
tinkerings, employment gaps, a stitched-up resumé, abject
confessions, letters of resignation, disability cheques —these
would be a few of the mainstays of getting by. And the
course of writing, if my younger self could have guessed it,
would have shocked and dismayed him too. Not the blaze
and burnout he, too neatly, pictured; but the daily filling,
like the stoking of a fire that cannot be allowed to go out, of

notebook after notebook, the notebooks stacked like bricks in a trunk that before long two men can barely lift; magazine publications sought relentlessly and eventually achieved in number, but also, discouragingly, by dint of numbers (one in twenty poems, one in ten stories the enduring average—making the achievement seem clerical-actuarial more than literary); a small press contract miraculously secured by twenty-six, then lost after a two-year wait; the first book not appearing until the author was forty-one, and only then thanks to an editor's determined battle with her colleagues; eventually, over the ensuing decade, five books to follow, a glad but still, somehow, a dubious victory, since all five books owed their public life, as the first one had, to the advocacy of a single unflagging editor, and none, despite prizes and some excellent reviews, sold more than two hundred and twenty copies, two less than half that. Perhaps, at highest estimate, nine hundred copies in total spread over the six books. A matter of embittered bafflement, wincing shame, or just, increasingly, numb resignation. This public side of writing sitting awkwardly with, indeed in debilitating contrast to, the private side of growing sureness of craft and accomplishment. None of that would have been remotely guessable to the twenty-four-year-old outpatient perched amid boxes in the middle of a boat riding dangerously low in the streaming current, mother scouting from the bow and father piloting behind, sighting the strange evidence of local flooding: splintered docks stranded in woods, cairns of debris on high ledges, sunken porches, trees with green leaves sailing by.

Twenty-six years later, in the summer of 2005, lowest water presented fewer interesting sights but greater dangers for navigation. The north end of Dry Pine Bay, with Meshaw Falls and Stony Rapids reduced to trickles of their usual selves, was now a mile-wide bed of shallows filled with weeds and barely submerged rocks. Far out from shore, still in the middle of the bay, I slowed to minimum speed and we putted toward the distant dock light of our camp, Heather leaning over the bow with the flashlight pointed down, expecting to hit rocks, as we had coming out, but trusting that the propellor would not break if we went slowly enough. Everywhere Heather swung her beam were weeds, swaying golden or yellow-brown or chartreuse in the light, with luminous murk between them, polleny clouds and bits and shreds of plant matter, and then the sudden rocks, looming up like the ridged brown backs of the snapping turtles, which had never failed to alarm me no matter how often I told myself that they were coming and I should expect them. As we picked our way toward shore, clunking unavoidably against some rocks, narrowly missing others, I found myself returned to another gingerly-taken trek across the bay, this time when it was frozen. It was another piece of the French River/Black River story I kept getting stuck on, but now that I come round to face it frankly, no invented character standing between myself and what happened, I find that, in terms of definite facts, there is not that much to relate. There is an abundance of mortar but too few bricks. And bricks are all I need just now.

CR The first or maybe second winter after they built their cottage, my parents wanted to try it out over Christmas. They were excited about the new venture and wanted to experience it in all seasons. They have always been such strong seizers of life. Zesty, appetitive, ambitious, energetic, strong, capable—all the robust adjectives I can assemble made them seem more indomitable and younger at forty, as they would have been then, than I was at forty or than any forty-year-old

I know. Age, gamely resisted, is only slowly eroding these qualities, and in some ways they still seem the youngest members of the family. (But I am filling in with mortar now, and I need to place just bricks.) The ice was thick all around the cottage, but the current of the main channel stayed open at the end of Four Mile Island, a black thread of water that ran across the bay, through the Swifts, and past the marina on its way to Recollet Falls and onward to Georgian Bay. Dad arranged with the marina owner to take us by boat to the end of the island; we would lug all of our stuff up the shoreline on toboggans. I remember being thrilled by the blackness of the water in the jagged seam that let us through, the whiteness of the snow on either side of it, and the chime-like tinkling of the broken ice against the sides of the marina owner's big metal boat. Everything sparkling; no one else about. I remember my parents grinning at each other, all of us grinning at each other, red-cheeked and puffing "smoke rings" that, in the frozen air, hung thickly for a moment, dense and solid-seeming as cotton balls.

I don't recall how many boat trips it took, but we didn't do things halfway. No pre-made meals or other short-cuts; we had everything we needed for the full Christmas dinner, with all the trimmings; gifts for the stockings (we might have left the bigger gifts behind); skates, hockey sticks, snowshoes, ice fishing gear—all that we required for the whole winter adventure. Everything is a marvel when your eyes are new and curious. Taking turns pulling the toboggan piled high with boxes, others at the side to steady the always about-to-topple load. Floundering through deep, white snow; Mom carrying Sarah, who would have been less than three. Dad and I chopping with axes at the ice, chopping and chopping—we had not thought of an ice auger—until the water bubbled through, strangely yellowish, like ginger ale, which I marvelled at, unable to reconcile it with the black water I had seen from the boat. Clearing a rink—hard, long work, this—and skating and skating over a surface that dwarfed our backyard rectangle, yet whose ice was strangely pebbled and rough, as though the impress of giant boot treads had hardened in it. Bobbing bait through holes that kept slushing over: no bites. Spotting animal tracks—rabbit, deer, fox, criss-crossing and overlapping as if in a chase game—clean as bite marks in white frosting.

It was all enormous fun. What did us in was the cold. We simply could not keep warm enough, and in the end that forced us to cut the trip short. The cabin sat up on concrete blocks and the north wind howled under the thin floorboards, keeping them icy. (The next summer we would seal off the exposed sides with stones and cement, which made it easier to heat, though we never tried another winter visit.) It was a prefab cabin, with thin cedar walls and large windows, designed for summer use. The electric baseboard heaters, even cranked up as high as they could go, took off just the worst of the chill. We stoked the fire day and night, but it warmed only a small circle in front of itself, which we took turns sitting in. Once when I was sitting there in a thick wool sweater, we smelled something burning which we couldn't place, until I turned around and everyone gasped at the orange ring smoldering on my back. We kept the oven on, whether cooking or not. Closed doors to every room except the ones we were in. Still, though we gained a few degrees, it was always possible to see your breath, at least a faint mist of it, inside. At night we all slept in two beds, four in one double bed and three in the other, trading places in what we called "musical beds," seeking a warmer niche we could never find, catching a few winks of sleep and then jarring awake again with the cold. By dawn there was a half inch of ice on the water in the big plastic garbage pail we had filled from the river and stood in the corner of the kitchen.

After two days my parents decided we should leave, not four or five days hence, as planned, but the next day, tomorrow. They said later, marvelling at the resistance of children, that none of us had complained and we were obviously having fun (as were they at times), but they just couldn't take any more shivering. But how to get a message to the marina owner to come early? We had no phone: to Dad, on call since his mid-twenties, no place could be a holiday where a phone might ring. We would have to cross the ice and find a house with a telephone.

I don't remember any discussion about who, or how many, should go. What would there have been to discuss? Mom's place was with the younger children, and mine, as eldest son, was always beside my dad. We set off up the shore, toques snugged down, boots laced up, faces wrapped with scarves, wearing as many layers of clothing as we could find. We should have worn less: it was warm work walking. I sensed Dad's nervousness and his uncertainty, which he seldom showed, about just where we might safely cross. Not here, he said, after we had stopped and sighted across; a little farther up. Then, when we had stopped again at the further point: Not quite here; just up ahead. He was trying to estimate what he could not know accurately: the safest point, the thickest ice, between where the main current weakened it to our left and where the still distant falls and rapids weakened it to our right. He expressed no doubt there was such a point; following in his footsteps—he kept telling me to stay well back—I felt anything but sure. I watched his back, glancing nervously at the white vista on either side. More and more I watched my feet. It is a frightening thing, but also of surpassing interest, to not know if the next step will support your weight. Among intellectual pursuits, only writing, I have found, carries a comparable charge of half-delicious dread. The ice creaked and groaned, squeaking at times like a rusty hinge, whether because it was about to break or as a natural breathing and stretching I had no idea. We stopped talking and were connected only by a shared tension, as the first shore fell far behind and the one ahead approached in tiny increments. Each shore was an impossible distance away now. It was the middle of the river. One hundred feet, or more, above the sturgeon settled in cold silt. Nothing but glittering white to either side, until the faint smudge of green at either end. Dry Pine Bay as I had never seen it before.

I remember no further details about the crossing, or about climbing the forested bluff on the other side, which must have been hard work, or about the long slog down through snowy woods to the marina or perhaps a closer inhabited house. The next thing I remember is Dad going through the ice. It happened when we were almost home, across the river and close to shore, perhaps two hundred yards from the cabin. We were exhausted, and much relieved; both feelings, he said later, caused him to relax his vigilance and miss the telltale bit of timber poking up through the snow, the corner of a dock or other structure which had weakened the ice around it. He went through instantly, with no cry, just a swooshing sound, and was floundering in the yellow water that looked like ginger ale with ice chunks floating in it. I shouted and rushed forward. Stay back, he rasped, Stay back. But as the hole widened, his heavy swipes batting off new chunks, I kept trying to come closer, from one angle then another, not having any idea how I could help him but needing desperately to try. But there was really nothing I could do except to watch him flounder, gasping and heaving in a strange, slow-motion way, until his feet found bottom—we were near shore, after all—and with a last, walrus-like lurch, he heaved up onto land and staggered to his feet. I ran in beside him. He looked down at me, his face bright red, and then we both looked down the shore at the cabin with the smoke curling out of its chimney. My relief at the sight was enormous, but he, inside the drenched clothes and with a doctor's knowledge, saw it differently. Hurry, he said hoarsely; hurry, now. And indeed, before we were halfway there his stride had become a weaving stumble, and then a robotic, stiff-limbed stagger; he looked not like my father at all but like a giant baby tottering, toppling forward, and when I tried to take some of his weight with my arm around his waist, he sagged for an instant into me and almost brought us both crashing down. He stumbled on, we both did, and somehow made it to the bottom of the cottage steps, where at last he let me hook my arm around his waist and help him climb. Glancing up at his face, I saw white frost around his eyes, almost sealing them shut, a face pink in places but mostly ashen-white.

And then we opened the door and saw mostly red. Greg had slipped while running across the floor and split his head open on the corner of a stool. Bright red blood was pooled on the kitchen floor, and Mom was holding him in her lap, a wash cloth filled with ice, soaked red and dripping, pressed tightly to his forehead. The other children were hanging back, as they had no doubt been told to do, clustering anxiously in the living room; but I was standing beside Dad in the doorway, and when Mom raised the wash cloth a moment to let him see, I saw the strange white gleam, like bone in steak meat, of my brother's skull. There would be no cosy wrapping of Dad in blankets by the fire, no near-miss story to spin out for the others—not yet. First there was medical work. But there was a necessary minimum of warming he had to do, especially of his hands, before he could trust them to function properly. All this must have passed between my parents in glances, for I remember no words spoken. They were good in a crisis. They shared that knowledge of themselves.

Sue and I were given the job of taking Chris and Sarah into the middle room and keeping them quiet there. None of us were to emerge, no matter what we heard, until it was over. That was not hard; it was a bit frightening, unnerving, but also grave and exciting, as all the trip had been. The solemn, big-eyed looks we traded as we huddled on the bed certified to ourselves that we were still on an adventure together, though now a sombre and fantastic one. Greg had been badly hurt, but not beyond our father's power to mend him. His piercing shrieks were a child's pure, uninhibited voicings of pain and terror. Some power of medical assessment, the gauge of an emergency's extent, must permeate a doctor's family, just as in a fisherman's family some capacity to measure an approaching storm must trickle down even to the youngest. Thus we knew somehow that our brother's screams—earsplitting, hair-raising though they were—were not that serious. Harder to bear—because I could not hear them well, just catching bits between the screams, when Greg paused momentarily to gulp down air—were my parents' murmured comments as they prepared to work. The voices sounded tense in these exchanges. Tense from worry? Cross? About what? Was it a real disagreement or just the friction of two working side by side under stress? I couldn't, from the fragments, make much sense of the cause of the crossness or worry. Something about *local*, or *no local*, which I knew meant anaesthetic—and then *suture? . . . wrong size* . . . . Somehow I got the sense that we were improperly equipped and that, because of this, unusual measures would have to be resorted to. That didn't seem possible, though. Thinking of our multiple toboggan trips up the shore, I couldn't believe that we could be lacking anything essential. I told myself I must have it wrong, I must not understand. Four years later, I would find myself lying on the same bed in the same room, my right shoulder dislocated after a waterskiing fall—my siblings must have been in another bedroom, keeping quiet again, all of them now old enough to do this without supervision—when I heard the same sorts of murmurings from the living room, murmurings of doubt and possible insufficiency. Snatches: . . . *haven't set a dislocation since* . . . *resident* . . . *Parry Sound's an hour away* . . . . And this time I knew exactly what was being debated in low voices—whether Dad was up to doing this himself, and whether it wouldn't be better to go to the marina and drive to the hospital in Parry Sound—and, shivering in my wet bathing suit, a crinkly pouch of loose skin where my shoulder bone had been—and knowing, furthermore, how the doubts would be decided—I expelled them from my mind forcibly. Dad and Mom came into the room, Dad with a hypo of Demerol, I think it was, and as he injected it, I remember thinking woozily that each year we were better supplied, but that the emergencies kept staying one year ahead of us . . . and then the slow warm wave of Demerol broke curling through me, dissolving pain and thought and most of doubt, the latter lingering only as a stiff tension in my arm—*Relax, now, you're going to have to relax*—as Dad picked it up and pinned my hand under his bicep.

And then it was over. My last memory of that Christmas trip, our one and only winter trip to French River, is of having a meal at the Voyageur Restaurant, just north of

Parry Sound, which used to be our stop on Highway 69. Three hours north of Hamilton, it was our breakfast pit stop when we left at dawn; if we had stopped there now, only an hour into the drive home, perhaps it was in celebration of the dangers we had survived, the collisions with disaster we had avoided. We may all, our parents in particular, have felt that now the cottage was truly ours. For that is another important part of the cottage myth: the place of manageable perils, the kind that with fortitude you can overcome and feel comforted for having done so. The Voyageur, which is gone now, replaced by the Wendys-Tim Hortons pairing that dominates the highways, had a tall red conical top, like a huge dunce cap or construction zone marker, that looked slightly ridiculous but could be seen a long way off. There was the usual clamour and excitement among the kids of ordering in a restaurant, but a special mood of festivity seemed to brighten our table this time. My parents kept glancing and smiling at each other. Their looks had the warm intensity, brimming with shared knowledge, that cannot be feigned and that only the most tightly bound couples acquire. Their gazes locked in a circle of two so charmed and so desirous of being complete in itself that its inhabitants would always have a hard time seeing when the circle was neither charmed nor complete and when in fact it depended on the charms of others to complete it.

CR Our Christmas at French River. Really a rather simple story, after all. Almost, if its lines could be kept clean and uncluttered, the kind of story, of danger gamely met and surmounted by a family, that used to be featured, and probably still is, in *Reader's Digest* as a True Life Adventure. Except that, over the years, whenever I tried to tell it—or the story of Mrs. V.'s drowning, which got attached to and confused with it, as if they were two parts, or two versions, winter and summer, of the same story—or when I tried to tell any other story of Black River, or French River, or whatever river it originally was—I felt the weight, the oppressive intricacy, of family history bear down upon me, so many layers of secrets and half-acknowledged or unacknowledged truths, like fossil-laden strata of ancient rock, or the innumerable crystal featherings of ice and snow that accumulate to form a glacier . . . that in the end the story was just too massive to relate. It crumbled under its own weight, splintered, sank like a wreck out of sight. There were other problems in the telling, too. Some more devious, sly elves tinkering with the works. I came upon one by accident the other day, when I was thinking about writing this and had already started making—yet again—notes toward it.

There is a tiny handmade book, not five inches square, that sits beside my desk all the time. Heather produced it for her bookmaking class at the Ontario College of Art & Design. It is a beautiful little thing: board covers surfaced with pink handmade paper, with a black spine; no lettering on the outside, just the embossed pink convolutions of a rosebud; inside, "The Rosebud," one of the shortest of the tales collected by Jacob and Wilhelm Grimm, is hand-printed and illustrated by Heather's spare and delicately evocative line drawings in black ink. The tale is so short it can be repeated here in its entirety: *There was once a poor woman who had two little girls. The youngest was sent to the forest every day to gather wood. Once when she had gone a long way before finding any, a beautiful little child appeared who helped her to pick up the wood and carried it home for her. Then in a twinkling he vanished. The little girl told her mother, but the mother wouldn't believe her. Then one day she brought home a rosebud and told her mother the beautiful child had given it to her and said he would come again when the rosebud opened. The mother put the rosebud in water. One morning the little girl didn't get up out of bed. The mother went and found the child dead, but looking very lovely. The rosebud had opened that same morning.* I have enjoyed this story, and the book Heather has made of it, countless times, but the other day, while I was turning its pages again, something caught at me that I had never noticed before. Even in such a short story, something alters mysteriously between its beginning and its end. "Two little girls" are mentioned at first, a number that is reinforced by the use of "The youngest" right after. But why should there be two little girls when the story only concerns one and the other is never even mentioned again? Carelessness on the part of the storyteller? A meaningless adornment? But we are told, and it seems likely, that such folk tales, through their innumerable retellings, get pruned of all extraneous elements. The best way I can understand this is that the two children are actually one child, and so even is the "beautiful little child" she meets in the forest, a magical alter ego. The storyteller is tugged between everyday realism and psychic truth. In two spots, for the space of two letters, the magical forest being becomes a "he," but this masculine gender twinkles out of sight behind the being's other evocations as a "beautiful little child," and again, a "beautiful child," epithets which accord with the dead girl "looking very lovely." Her poor peasant self and magical forest self have, in death, fused into one. An analogous splitting and fusing must have happened in the mind of the storyteller: an intuitive understanding of doubleness on the psychic or magic plane, which—in obedience to narrative or, perhaps more, psychological needs—could become a literal doubleness in order to establish, for teller and listener, a safe fallback position in consensual reality. What clinical psychology calls dissociation becomes, in the psychology of narrative, something more like re-association: elements of the psyche become different and discrete characters, which fuse again at crucial moments of change. The splitting into separate selves that can act independently and interact with one another seems necessary to make transformation possible, just as the fusing, or at least forgetfulness at times of the characters' separateness, is the storyteller's implicit acknowledgement that all this, and all these, form a magical play within a single psyche.

Something like this must have happened to me when I tried to tell the Black River stories. I was a while recalling this, or recognizing it, partly because it has been so long since I last tried to write those stories. I abandoned the attempt, all the attempts (the trunk they filled stays locked in another room)—though they nagged at me sometimes. In most of my stabs at writing the story of the winter trip there was a suspenseful scene in which Greg nearly fell through the ice in a game of crack the whip. This scene, with its climax of the one child cracked off the whip toward the ragged hole of open black water, became central to the story. Sometimes the other parts disappeared and it became the whole story. I, as eldest and strongest, was on the other end of the whip from Greg, the heaviest pivot about which the others would spin and skim and fly. We went out to the rim in order of age and size, or we started to: after me there was Sue, then Chris; but then there was a transposition of the youngest, Sarah, for Greg. This produces a pleasing symmetrical alternation of genders—boy, girl, boy, girl, boy—while also placing Greg, my double, nearest the open hole. How parsimonious imagination is in changing just the one detail needed. We did skate, on rough pebbly ice we had cleared the snow from; Dad did fall through a hole in the ice; and Greg did fall and split his head open—but a middle element was needed, a near-miss uniting the two hits so to speak, and imagination provided it so persuasively that when I think of the three events—two real: Dad's fall, Greg's fall; and one imaginary: Greg's near-fall (snatched back, or pulled out, by a mighty effort on my part, though the most important image was the helpless speeding before the plunge)—the memories have exactly the same weight, the same texture of reality in my mind. Or no, not quite the same: it is the smoothness and clear vividness of the made-up scene that differentiate it from the fragmentary glimpses, blurry discontinuities, of the memories of events I know actually occurred. When I wanted to, I could sort this out; I could separate the middle term—"middle" in the sense of pattern, of a necessary bridge—and distinguish fact from fiction. But I seldom made the effort to do so, and when I did, the story, curiously, seemed to lose something that belonged to it. Even now, when I am trying to rid myself of my Black River vampire by telling only what I know, I feel strong inner resistance at erasing this invented bit. By now—such is the power of story—it seems false in a way to do so, a betrayal of the truth to some crude inventory of the facts.

Why? One thing I have learned from my years of writing, a bit of practical tradecraft, is that the more stories want to stay partial and shift their parts, the more important it becomes to take note of which parts never change. Through all the years, in all the versions of the Black River story, wearing its winter or summer face, there had to be a woman who drowned and there had to be a hole in the ice that someone who looked a lot like me was about to fall into.

ଔ   At last Heather and I had threaded our way through the field of rocks, and the weeds had given way to slightly deeper water below the white spill of the falls. Crossing this pool before the dock, the black water shimmering from the light over the boathouse, we skirted a group of mallards feeding, a hen and several of her young, dipping their heads in the current and swallowing what they found. They seemed unbothered by us, placidly paddling a few feet farther away as we passed. Tying up, I asked Heather to shine the flashlight down into the water. She knew what I was looking for. She had heard Dad's stories of fishing as a boy on White Lake, near Ottawa, where his lifelong fishing mania had begun, and where the pickerel had been so plentiful, apparently, that a light shone from the dock at night would pick out rows of their glittering, faceted, jewel-like eyes. We did see a few gleams and glints, but nothing resembling eyes.

Hand in hand, we walked up the dirt road to our cabin at the top of the hill. Past the boathouse, on flat rock next to the road, was a low stone and cement wall built in a tight circle, like a turret lopped off at waist height. Inside the wall was a surprisingly deep hole, almost twenty feet deep, smooth-sided like a drilled well. It was a "swirl hole" made by a black ball of granite (it looks like a bowling ball in the photographs in local history books) churning around and around in a forceful eddy. This would have been in the times of glacial melting, when the river was much higher and the falls poured over the entire point. In the older history books there is no protective wall in the pictures, just people standing beside the hole looking down, posed in attitudes of curious amazement, the retrieved rock in the foreground. The wall was built decades ago by the present camp owner, either because a child had fallen in or because a child could fall in—the story, which was a minor attraction of the place, kept changing, perhaps in accordance with what the teller thought the listener wished, or could stand, to hear.

I unpacked some of the presents I had received and then decided to leave the rest till morning. I felt exhausted, emptied out by the business of turning fifty. It felt like a pointless odyssey, I told Heather, like I'd spent a long hard day and all I'd done was go from this end of the bay to the other and back. Sometimes it takes all day just to do that, she replied. And if she, or I, did not say exactly those things, they are exactly the kinds of things we both would say. I felt utterly spent as I swallowed the pills I take nightly, knowing that the usually lengthy process of falling asleep is even longer, sometimes much, much longer after a family visit.

Lying in bed, we made a game of picking out shapes and figures we could find in the dark and light wood fibres of the chipboard walls and ceiling. It was yet another version of the ancient human drive to make meaning out of chaos, to find the recognizable, the important, the useful, in wisps of cloud, in veins of rock, in scattered pinpricks of light. Heather said she saw a face, a head, repeating in the different chipboard sheets around the room. At first I couldn't see it, even with her pointing, but then I did. She was right: it did look a little like a weird old man, and also like a gaping infant, and the combination was, as she said, creepy. This bald gnome—just its head—stared down at us from all sides and above, and as I stared back at it, I felt a stab of recognition. I had seen it before, but I was a few minutes remembering where and when. It was the climax of a nightmare I had, one of a series of recurring dreams I had during my first year out of hospital, terrifying grotesques that I called my "ward dreams," which seemed less like returns to the actualities of the ward and more like repeated attempts to somehow encompass the experience, to find an image that could stand for all its inchoate horrors. In the dream I was in two, or maybe three, places at once. I was searching in a raging blizzard for something that was lost. I was panting and plunging, hunting frantically in a frenzy of white that offered no tracks or clues. As I ploughed through drifts of snow, eyes slitted against the driving ice pellets, I could hear the lost thing crying, a pitiful mewing that sounded barely human. Amid the blizzard's shrieks and howls, the sound seemed to come from here, then there, then . . . . Then I was home, warm in my bed with the covers pulled up, listening to the storm rage all around the house, the wind moaning, snow and ice scattering like hurled seed against the sides and roof. I was content for a time, but then—I was aware of something coming. Closer. Closer. I could feel its approach, out there in the howling dark of the blizzard, but I did not know how it could be making its way so purposefully toward me. The dream ended with a moment of classic horror: I threw open the door to see the ice-covered screaming face of the fetus I had left to freeze, and at the same instant I knew that the abandoned creature was myself. The shrieking homunculus was both pre-birth and post-death; in the knitting magic of dream, it could, like the similar figure in Munch's *The Scream*, howl with both throttled hope and ancient misery, an accusatory wail that echoed from before the beginning and long after the end. I woke with a wild shout, sweating and thrashing. It was the worst of the ward dreams, the climax of them, as if the dream-maker had finally set his guns and found the range. Soon after it, I began to sleep a little better, and to settle a little less provisionally into the life I was remaking in a rented room and a part-time job as a dish-washer.

That—the searing freeze frame of nightmare—was not the image I wanted to start my fifty-first year on. It could hardly help my sleep, which was as hard as ever to come by and which I needed more and more. Heather had turned on her side and was beginning to breathe deeply, entering her rest. I let my mind wander and drift. What I found myself remembering—surprisingly, for one who was so tired of travelling—was our boat ride down Dry Pine Bay, in mid-afternoon, to attend the party. I remembered the sensations of skimming in bright sunlight over sparkling blue water, trying to summon an ebullience and a blood-warmth that would match the red T-shirt I was wearing, spotting, when we were still far out from shore, the bright ovals of balloons and the paler ovals of faces gathered in the clearing. I wondered if they felt some anxiety as they watched the spot of red get bigger as it approached. Would he—would I—be up to it, after all? Would the party come off, would it be a success? From the back of the boat I had been able to project myself forward, beyond the weeds, into the clearing, and imagine how we looked speeding toward them. Now, thinking back, I could occupy that vantage point, or the one I had actually occupied as driver, my hand on the throttle; and a third that seemed to drift skyward so it could take in both boat with couple and waiting partyers, and, drifting even higher, the river on which they had shared so much history. Lying in a rented room, Heather asleep beside me, feeling relieved to be fifty at last rather than turning fifty, I could imagine it all, I could go anywhere without even getting out of bed.

Leavetaking

Psychotherapy, like other works of the imagination, evolves by taking note of repetitions and trying to situate these in a larger design. Attending to the clamour of a life, the listener—or listeners, once therapist and patient are working together—pick out recurrent themes and motifs, which can function as heralds, reminders, touchstones, warnings, puzzles, goals—all of these, in the strongest cases. Such a leitmotif was the word "leavetaking," which announced itself to me shortly before the publication of *Contrary Angel*, my fourth book, and which has figured centrally or peripherally in all my meetings with Dr. George in the year and a half since then.

As the time approached to launch the new collection of stories, Heather and I decided to organize the event ourselves. No more being shoehorned into a bill of two or three or five other authors, each performing from the podium for fifteen minutes in an exuberant attempt to claim attention for his or her book; with the family and friends each had brought out sitting in clearly marked camps with unoccupied chairs between them, loudly applauding and cheering their champion's efforts and sullenly enduring the others'; the cheese and cracker trays sparsely picked at, and the cheap wine in plastic glasses downed only because it was free and alcoholic—no, this time we would take a break from all that. We would do it up right. A good rented space (not a loaned one that was free for obvious reasons), good food and drink, our own music, people we wanted to be there. Yes, for once. Yes! We became excited thinking about it.

The lightheartedness was partly determined, an offset to the heavy drag I felt increasingly in my literary endeavours (though not yet, thankfully, in the writing itself). Literary in-siders—booksellers, publishers, writers—sometimes talk of the 500 readers a small press book can expect to find in Canada. The 500, they will say, with a smile or shrug depending on their mood. Hearing this I have to resist the impulse to wince. My three previous books had sold a total of 500 copies *between* them, so if dropping another book into the world was not going to be an occasion to hang crape it had better be an occasion to hang bunting. Yes, it would put us in the hole—about 700 dollars, we estimated, even if the publisher kicked in a bit—but if the book sold 350 copies (and hope, amnesiac as ever, was rising to that level), we could still break even. What difference did it make? Had it ever even remotely been about the money? The main significance of breaking even, a point I clung to out of pride, was that earning anything, even one dollar, put me outside the camp of vanity publishing. One book, after greater than usual expenses in its preparation—multiple copyings and expedited mailings, photographic development—had netted, as I calculated one day on the back of an envelope, twenty dollars. So? The book, another handsome one, was out there; or it existed anyway, and in much spiffier form than as a three-ring binder in my room. Someone else had paid to make this happen, and had thrown in a free lunch besides. A labour of love—what else could you call it? On saner days it is more than enough.

We wanted to make it a party more than a literary event. A cocktail party briefly interrupted by a reading, was how I put it—the reverse of the usual. Asking around, we found 424, an event venue at that address on Wellington Street. Inspecting the premises one spring morning, led around by Elisabeth, the owner, we liked what we saw. A large, orange-brick Victorian house, an entrance of double wooden doors. A generous vestibule opening, on either side, into long spacious rooms for entertaining. Wide stairs rose from the vestibule to an outside deck, lovely, Elisabeth said, if the night was warm. Long wooden tables, with armchairs and settees, in the room where we would lay out the buffet; a kitchen in back with wide steel counters for prepping the food, which we had decided to make ourselves (as we had done at our wedding, nine years before). The other room had a grand piano at one end (No, we didn't think anyone would be playing); at the other end, a bar with stamped-tin front and sides, bluish lighting around the bottles and glasses, and a sound system for our CDs; halfway down the room, a large aquarium inset in one wall (only a few pale goldfish in all that water, the survivors, Elisabeth said, of a recent piscine plague and die-off), and a few round tables with stools against the other wall.

Space. Cool and tranquil (with the bluish light, the bubbling aquarium). Dimly-lit, even in daytime: we would bring our own standing lamp for my fifteen-minute reading.

We made the invitations at home—printed on rectangles of velum with a vaguely floral pattern reminiscent of Morris wallpaper, then glued to cardboard—and mailed them to about three dozen people. Again, if most of them came, the party would be about the same size as our wedding reception, with a core group of the same people: minus a few relatives, plus a few friends we had made in Toronto. It felt, curiously, like a wedding, too: a celebration to mark the end of one phase, the beginning of another. Just what the phases were, I wasn't sure. The approaching event felt festive and elegiac, both, with one emotion coming to the forefront then the other.

It was during this busy time, which coincided with our getting ready to move to a new apartment, that I first heard a voice say *leavetaking*. In a movie, to convey the quality of voice I heard, they would probably use a voice-over and have the actor do a little double take, glancing around to see who else had heard it. I had heard this voice (though not this particular message) a few times in my life, separated by long intervals. It was like the voice of someone standing very close and uttering the three syllables matter-of-factly—not whispering, not murmuring, but also, above all, not insisting—simply stating unequivocally. The question of obedience does not come up with such a voice. It is not a voice that can be argued with, reasoned with; it does not invite, even remotely, those appeals. It is the voice that knows, knows beyond doubt, and will do no more than declare what it knows. It is not a voice that speaks often: there is no need to squander its authority in situations where ordinary inner promptings and reasoning can work out a course of action.

Leavetaking, it said. Never more, never less. I was to hear it every day, at least once and usually many times, for the next eighteen months. Never was there the slightest alteration in either the content or the tone of the message—a calm and unflagging persistence that amazed me sometimes, without ever really surprising me. Nothing that could speak in that voice was going to leave without getting what it had come for.

ᘒ The launch was scheduled for June 1, 2004. I brought up *leavetaking* at my next meeting with Dr. George, a psychiatrist I had been seeing about twice a month since the end of the previous December. The visits meant an inconvenient, hour-long drive back to my hometown of Hamilton, but they were worth it. Dr. George, who, better than any other doctor I have met, balances her human responsiveness with her professional responsibilities, asked me if I thought leavetaking meant suicide. I told her it was one of the word's possible meanings but in this case it did not seem uppermost. Why? The voice that spoke the word was dark with intent, darkly mysterious, whereas the counsellors of suicide I have heard have been matter-of-fact. They are the ultimate problem solvers. They are all business.

Dr. George looked at me for a few moments. "But you said the voice was blank, expressionless. Not mysterious." She has an excellent memory. She took detailed notes during our first few meetings but has seldom needed to since.

I took a slow, deep breath through my nose; something I do more often, or am more aware of doing, in her office. "In tone, yes. But . . . what's more mysterious than a blank? Especially a repeated one."

"You have to fill it in."

"Yes. I think so. I don't think I'm going to get much choice."

Dr. George said nothing for a time. She has a quiet, comforting demeanor, but within that you sense a mind of great quickness, alert to small shifts and the way these can change a larger pattern that is assembling. We had snagged on something—we both knew that. *Leavetaking* was more than a word puzzle. It would not be confined to those sorts of rules and stakes. Dr. George let our mutual awareness of this percolate through the silence a little longer, before asking, "What else can you say about this voice?"

"Sometimes I think of it in theatre terms. You're watching these endless scenes inside your mind, the mental stage. Conversations of every kind, scenes, tableaux—the cast of thousands . . . with music, sound effects, lighting . . . all of it. Some scenes you're in, others you're just watching. But sometimes you catch a comment from below—that's my sense of the direction, though in the theatre image it would be further back, behind. Someone out beyond the stage action, in the dark, unseen. Someone—the director maybe —watching from the back of the theatre. 'Notes,' I've heard actors call these comments."

Getting no comment from Dr. George, who was just listening with a thoughtful expression, I went on, elaborating a classification or hierarchy of voices. The points reeled out like lines of a lecture I didn't know I had written. There are voices that are clearly external. They come from lovers, friends, family members, politicians, celebrities, passersby. They speak to us across the whole range of human intensity and intention, and we listen (or not) and respond (or not) from no less rich an array of possibilities. There are other voices that are just as clearly internal. These voices, multitudes of them, form the monologues, dialogues and choruses of our mental conversations, our inner life. No matter how strident or otherwise urgent such voices become, still we can, unless we have crossed over into madness, retain an awareness that they have been generated from within, that they are products of our mind, bespeaking our myriad desires, questions, reasonings and frustrations. But there is a third kind of voice, heard still this side of madness, which, though it is heard and recognized internally, has something external, not-us, and peculiarly authoritative about it. It has so much authority, in fact, that it does not stoop to command. It states. It declares with calm certitude. It utters things in a flat tone, without overt emotion or emphasis.

Dr. George looked slightly quizzical by the time I had finished. Her faint frown and cocked head might have translated as: Sounds like a lot to load into a voice. A word.

"He may have confused himself with the owner of the theatre," I quipped.

"Well, we'll have to set him straight about that," said Dr. George brightly, with the buoyant touch, especially in closing, that is another indispensable part of her repertoire.

ଔ I had come to Dr. George as a refugee from psychiatry and anti-psychiatry. When I entered her office, on one of the last days of 2003, I was deeply depressed and, along with that, a part of it, simply worn out from the decades of crash and burn. The slide I was on was proving steeper and more protracted than in previous years. It looked like settling in. Three women close to me—Heather, my sister Sue, and my mom—had been pressuring me for months to take another chance on the medical system, to try again to find a decent doctor. My last regular visits to a psychiatrist had been in the early 1990s, after a mental storm of particular violence had swept away my three-year teaching career and left me on a long-term disability pension. The doctor I contacted then, who had treated me during my eighteen-month hospitalization a decade earlier, scored as 5, or "complete," the level of my disability on the insurance forms. He informed me that the initial diagnosis of schizophrenia had been wrong (as had been, therefore, the treatment—which he left unstated); my illness was manic depression or, as it was now called, bipolar affective disorder. Accordingly, we tried lithium, which coated my upper body and face with pimples and filled my mind with fog. Then, carbamazepine: fewer pimples, less severe fogging, but still those gaps, that milky mist to try to think through. Memory hitches; reaching for simple words. It was intolerable. We settled on a trial of clonazepam, a mild anticonvulsant with sedative properties (which, alas, would wear off) and an "anti-kindling" mechanism, not yet understood, that in some people helped to regulate the worst veering of moods. It was the mildest form of treatment possible for my condition, he said; he wouldn't prescribe it to anyone not sufficiently vigilant and self-aware—but he had one other patient getting by on just this drug. So I became his second. And stopped seeing him when I thought I could manage. He phoned the prescription refills to the pharmacy in the small town I was living in. Then a local GP started writing them. Word reached me that the psychiatrist had retired. Heather and I married and moved to Toronto. I picked up work, part-time at first, then more hours. The GP I found was visibly frightened by my psychiatric resumé; his eyes actually widened as he took the notes. (They would widen like that every time I saw him, even if it was just for a routine throat infection or bursitis.) It was the sheer incompetence of the shrink he referred me to, along with my accelerating slide toward a bottom I still couldn't imagine, that got me frightened enough, desperate enough, to listen to what the women in my life were trying to tell me.

Heather and I called my Toronto shrink The Idiot. I had been seeing him once a month for several years, whenever I needed my prescription refilled. He wouldn't phone it in to the pharmacy or write for more than one month: he wanted to bill for the office visit. The appointment lasted for half an hour. He spent at least half of that time, every time, finding my file folder, fixing his coffee and stirring it by the machine. Sometimes more time was wasted because he couldn't remember my name. He would come back with a file for Barrens, or Burnez, or Marks, or Michaels. He never did learn my name in the several years I saw him, and he mispronounced it each time I told it to him again. When I showed up for one appointment and the nurses said, with nasty looks, that he had moved—only one had any idea where his new office might be—I guessed that his privileges at that hospital had been suspended. He worked now in a little brick building over a pharmacy; he seemed to have cut a deal with the pharmacist, since he urged me to fill my prescriptions downstairs and sulked and made difficulties if I wanted to go elsewhere. He had the insufferable bombast of the dullard still vested with authority. After the 9/11 attacks, he treated me to a thirty minute harangue on Egyptian politics; that was the price of pills that day. He raised the dosage as I requested—as I increasingly needed—but asserted his authority by lecturing me on my condition, making inane speculations, sometimes rationalizing his own laxness by flattering himself for having the sagacity to know when a patient was capable of self-monitoring. But eventually, if you have been seeing for years a doctor you call The Idiot, you have to ask yourself: Who is? Seeing a doctor you find contemptible is a position of the utmost precariousness. He broke most of the ethical rules of psychiatry, but that wasn't what scared me most about him. What frightened me was that I could wind up in hospital under his care, and then he would have the power to do as he saw fit with me. I knew more than a little about what that could mean.

A mark of my good beginning with Dr. George was that we wasted not five seconds on that parody of a physician. He vanished like the zephyr he was. I rambled my history—by now a long story to get out, even sketchily, in an hour—while she took notes and asked pertinent questions.

She agreed to begin seeing me (for reasons I still don't know and would like to ask her about sometime), though her focus now was on community outpatient services and she had a dwindling private practice. She made three things very clear in that first session. She knew the relevant drugs and felt confident that there was one that could help, but she would not insist on that aspect of things. "I'm here to advise. The decisions are yours." She expressed admiration for the toughness and resilience I had shown in getting this far on my own; the resourcefulness with which I had assembled such a panoply of survival tactics; all the tricks and muscles I had developed to get by. But—the other side of her admiration—she was not content with what she perceived as my fatalism, my resigned acceptance of getting by as my allotted ceiling.

"I think you can feel much better. And I know you deserve to."

It was a hard message to hear in some ways. The tears that started to my eyes felt like droplets of rain after a massive drought. Were they harbingers of the real downpour needed, or just a tantalizing sprinkle?

೦೩ That water image—the question of rain—makes me aware of a synchronicity that had somehow slipped my notice. Two weeks after that first visit with Dr. George, I began writing poems again. The closeness of the two events is so obvious to me now that I am amazed I ever overlooked it. Starting from my first discharge from hospital, in 1979, I had written poems by the hundreds, perhaps thousands—the one rough count I tried, the journals heaped around me on the mattress, I got lost and stopped around 1500—but the last poem had been almost a decade ago. They just stopped coming. A new aperture, or frequency, had opened up; and what came through on this new re-ceiver took the form of fiction. Since my first book of po-ems (a sampling from those thousands), I had published a book of stories and a novel; another of each was on the way. I missed poems, but when I tried to write one now, it died or turned into a story. Over time I stopped trying.

Then, on the morning of January 16, 2004, as I sat in the waiting area of a car repair shop, I opened my journal and wrote three poems. They came as they had before: unbidden, exhilarating; an unreeling of finished lines that made my hand ache to keep up with them. Drained, afterwards. And pleased, but puzzled: were the three an anomaly? A blip? No. They kept coming. Ten more in the last two weeks of Janu-ary. Forty-three more in frantic February. Nineteen in March. Apart from two blank months—a black slate of ex-haustion scrawled with moving chores—the poems came more or less continuously until the following January, when, almost as abruptly as they had started, they stopped, slackening over a few days then shutting off. I have written only a few since.

After March of that hectic year, when I felt myself sinking again, Dr. George made a surprising suggestion: Why not try writing a poem when I did not feel impelled to? This I resisted strongly. We had been dealing with the other dangers of my ten-week ride of mania: the sleep deprivation (two or three tossing hours, then back scribbling), the bad driving (speeding and scribbling, split-second swerves), the jangled, jumped-up nerves—a pause in the poems was not a top priority, even for me. Besides, my credo had always been "never write unless you have to." I had to let the wave crash into me and take dictation right from the curl. Speed was the essence of it: several minutes to draft a poem, several hours for a story, several weeks for a novel. Any other method—and I had tried some, hopefully—had resulted in faint, sterile productions. Lifeless, lily-livered things. Why mess with the two speeds I operated in: flat-out, overdrive; or motorless, up on blocks? I envied the steady producers: Graham Greene's "500 words a day." It sounded sane, as serene as writing ever could be. But it was nothing I could emulate. Besides, things got done my way. Done, done, and done.

But Dr. George, a bit like an oldtime Zen master, I see now, with their legendary whacks upside the head, likes to jar established habits of thought and action; shake "gotta be" routines out of their tracks. She is a believer in mind and spirit following behavior; lagging a little, reluctant disciples, but coming along in the end.

In a spirit of experiment, not expecting much, I continued to sit down to write poems, even when I had no strong desire to do so. It was one of the many "what if" or "as if" experiments I tried under Dr. George's guidance. To my surprise, this approach resulted in another twenty-one poems in April and a further seven in May. It could be done, I reported back, though the results were workmanlike efforts, not bad but a bit flat, and certainly not up to what I had written in the first flurry of the winter. Dr. George did not dispute this (good therapists, like good generals, must develop a fine sense of when ground can be ceded for now and when a position must be taken and secured); what mattered, she said, was that I had tried a working rhythm that lay somewhere between fever pitch and paralysis.

It is only now, almost two years later, that I discover the second result of the experiment, its even more surprising lesson. Working with an editor in England, I have been assembling a selection of the best poems from that poem-filled year ("a year in poems" or "a year in the life of the poem" were two subtitles I toyed with briefly). The contents, which are close to being finalized, include six poems from February and five from April. Out of a mood of wild euphoria and one of mild depression: almost exactly the same number of hits. And, if the pools of possibles from which these poems were chosen are compared—forty-three to twenty-one—then a better hit rate, indeed almost twice as good, from dogged pursuit as opposed to mad scramble. Even now, something in me rebels at it, suspects it as an actuarial perversion. It gives me pause. And that—pause, in all its (possibly healing) dimensions—is exactly what I think Dr. George hoped it would give me.

To venture an aphorism that Dr. George, more pragmatic and less high-flown, would not attempt but might approve: Being at the mercy *of* means denying the mercy *in*. That is as true of the mind as of any other tyrant.

So many of the poems in A *Thaw Foretold* evoke the poignancy of "as if": rites enacted at the threshold of change. Change wished for, prayed for, courted, celebrated, endured, lamented. The possibility of change approaching, passing (almost!), receding. Several of the poems speak from the afterlife: what more ultimate vantage of transition is there? Above all, the poems are infiltrated by water, the changing element. Black water seeps down to the dreams flowing between a sleeping couple; a sudden storm surrounds another stranded pair with teeming white veils, before snatching one of them with a lightning fork. A diver plunges into fathomless dark in search of rumored treasure; a bird cocks its head from an ice-coated window sill; a woman smiles at a photographer from a rickety wooden bridge over a waterfall. A man chops at thick ice, scenting a thaw; a man falls through weakened ice on a routine crossing. There is loss (and eventual recovery) at sea; there is passage across the river. A "seeping of crazed rains" is needed to nourish the honey locust. Clear water gives way to swamp, it becomes blood. Dependent swimmers cling to each other. Water hisses and crackles, becoming another element entirely: consuming fire. Deserts, the antitype of water, stretch out in boundless grains. An oasis, or mirage, is sighted. Rain falls.

ଔ Rain fell in sheets the night of my book launch; all day, as we ran our errands and prepared, the air had been humid and threatening. But the downpour helped to create the homey, cocktail party atmosphere we had envisioned. The dripping coats in the vestibule, the jumble of drying umbrellas. The rain that fell on the roof and off the eaves enveloped the proceedings in a softly sluicing, shushing sound. It snugged down the evening's hat brim and turned up its collars. People wandered about the spacious rooms while the music played, drinks in hand, sampling the food, meeting and chatting and laughing as we had hoped they would. My parents were there, my two sisters. A couple of old friends, a few new ones. Two or three writers I had met along the way and, over time, grown close to. An editor who had given me much support and friendship. A few of Heather's colleagues from the art store. When I gave my reading—just fifteen minutes, as promised—I was seated on a stool between the bar and the aquarium, the guests gathered in a close circle that took me all the way back to storytime in kindergarten. There was that same sense of drawing in to hear, of speaking the words intently. The whole evening, actually, was charged with that kind of nostalgia, something elegiac that was part of the festivity, a sense of finality, of something ending that—for me—hovered over all my encounters, imbuing them with a poignancy that threatened at times to become overwhelming. I did not know where this powerful sense of ending had come from, or to what precisely it referred. This ended a chapter—that much, that only, I knew. The people I had gathered around me on this evening were the ones I would invite—were, in many cases, the ones I *had* invited—to my wedding; they were also the ones that would be expected to attend my funeral.

And, of course, lest I forget that final aspect of things, I had that clear commentator to remind me at regular intervals: *leavetaking.*

The evening wound down in classic fashion, a few of the longest-known sipping Scotch and talking over the bartender's closing-time clanks and rinsings. Walking out after midnight into moist spring air, I recalled another discharge, in sunshine after recent rain, after a midnight of another kind, in another, long-ago-now spring. I cocked my head slightly, but was not really surprised when the voice remained silent. It spoke, I was learning, with a kind of ultimate economy, never deploying its word if its meaning was self-evident.

CR After that, Dr. George and I dug more determinedly into the possible meanings of leavetaking. We had to: I was hearing it all the time. *Leavetaking. Leavetaking. Leavetaking.* I began to see the word as something of a grindstone I was being sharpened against. But to what end? I remembered my dad's old whetstone in his tackle box; it was a dull, soft gray, saddle-shaped from the blades that had abraded its middle; when Dad had finished his slow circular pushings of the knife, on first one side then the other, the result was an implement that could free a fish from its flesh so slickly it drew only thin seams of blood.

While Dr. George listened, occasionally offering a comment or question, I followed the word's associations where they led me. I began to appreciate the cunning of the word. Not the frank goodbye, not the operatic farewell; leavetaking could encompass those, but it could suggest other things too. You could roam in this word, and I did. Usually its two halves seemed to want to reverse themselves. Taking leave: departure, permission, respite. In many of its permutations it seemed eager to add on a preposition and other words, as some chemical elements, oxygen for example, are avid to take on electrons and combine with other atoms. Take leave to—what did that mean? Venture to? Presume to? Take leave of—take leave of what? Of whom? Take leave of . . . one's senses! (We both laughed out loud at that. Neither of us had lost the sense of fun in our trades.) Strange, suggestive, parentheses-pregnant things occurred by the insertion of a space between the two nouns in the compound: Leave taking. Leave (the realm of) taking. Leave (off) taking. Leave (while (still)) taking.

This sleuthing took on a darker, more sinister edge when I started seeing what we referred to as my "ticket taker" or "train station" scenario. It was as if the director of Leavetaking—or was he the playwright?—had hit on a visual to go with his one-word script. By "seeing" I don't mean a dream or hallucination; it was something between the two, but verging on the latter. That is, I knew it came from my imagination, from my mind, but it had a force—an intention even—that seemed independent of me. It could intrude itself at any time, with such palpable reality that other thoughts and images popped like bubbles before it. I would sense—almost feel—an area of muddy grayness to my right—it was always to my right—and, without turning, I would be in it and seeing what it contained. A dim and grimy railway platform, deserted except for myself and one other figure standing close to me. He is dirty, dishevelled, with a face whose features stay in shadow, wearing a long, dark greatcoat filthy with use—all of his characteristics put him in the tradition of Gogol, Dostoyevsky, the Chekhov of "Ward No. 6" or "In the Ravine," or even Tolstoy if one recalls, from *Anna Karenina*, the little train station peasant who is usually associated with striking iron, whom Anna sees on arriving in Petersburg just after a watchman has been run over, sees (while on a train) in a vision at the edge of sleep as she is falling in love with Vronsky, and sees in the instant she throws herself under the wheels. My man is shabbier than Anna's muzhik; he looks even harder used, like a homeless man, a street person. Yet his seediness does not suggest weakness; indeed, he emanates an air of aggression, of confrontation. He does not extend his hand to demand what he wants because he does not need to; figuratively, the hand is always out there. He wants what I owe him, the money for the trip.

No, not little either, I told Dr. George when she asked for more details about the figure. He was my size, my build (at its thinnest and most gaunt); I knew the face in the shadows would be mine if I could see it. I may have hedged slightly in describing this figure for Dr. George, perhaps because he seemed clearly to embody the one meaning of leavetaking I had ruled out—in what amounted to a promise—at the beginning of our exploration. But Dr. George was not fooled. She was frowning slightly, at my ticket taker or at the power I had invested him with. He was my illness, the sickest part of me; we both knew that. And what did he trade in, what currency had he ever honoured, except mayhem? Now he had come to collect the rest of the fare. It was time to punch the last ticket.

This fit, all too neatly, into the tiredness I had been complaining of for months. This was core tiredness, a sense of utter depletion, of having reached the end. The well so drained, the stone at the bottom had cracked from dryness. It felt like an exhaustion of the spirit more than of the body or even, quite, of the mind. The rare good night of sleep refreshed muscles and even mood but did nothing to touch this emptying. Good days or bad days, bounces of good luck or bad, were irrelevant to it. As an aquifer replete with groundwater might belie a parched surface above it—so I explained to Dr. George, who by now was used to my thinking predominantly in metaphors, hopping from one to the other as a frog might use lily pads to cross a pond—so might a drained aquifer mock a landscape sparkling with rivulets from a recent shower. It felt, obviously, like terminal fatigue. The end of the line (as my ticket taker, who now appeared sometimes together with *leavetaking*—image and audio geared on the reel—was there to remind me).

One positive aspect of all this was the weird pungency—a powerful, aching poignancy—that came from thinking of each time as the last time. Each encounter was invested with a sorrowing potency. Moments glittered in harrowing, splendid isolation. I gave a reading in Hamilton in that state. I knew—not thought, not wondered if—*knew* it would be my last time reading from my work. Each word came out as if I had sown, tended, harvested, milled and baked it for the occasion. I heard, as if from faraway, sobbing at times while I was reading. When it was over, I stepped back from the microphone stunned, lightheaded, as if I might keel over. One of the other authors got up from his seat to shake my hand in the aisle; so did one of the booksellers hosting the event. Afterward, I sat with Heather for an hour in the car behind a Tim Hortons, drinking bottled water and cups of tea, trembling all over like a marathon runner (the passage had been about one) who had left it all on the track. It was one in the morning before I could trust myself to drive.

ℭ   Dr. George wasn't a fan of no-future-land. (Or of the type of driving that might be permitted in it. "Are you all right to drive?" she asked me at the end of many sessions at this time.) She didn't, couldn't, believe in it; but also, she didn't altogether buy that I believed in it. Especially since I was still insisting that suicide was not the end I saw, sensed, felt approaching.

"You're not making those kinds of plans? I have to ask."

I thought about it. I wanted to give her, always, a real answer.

"No, I'm not. In some ways that's the strangest part. I'm very close to the end. I can feel it. It's right here with me all the time. But . . . I don't know how it's going to be. I can't . . . quite see it."

"What about the new apartment? The painting you've done . . . every wall in it, multiple coats. The furniture you've bought. It sounds more like someone who's decided he deserves a future. A more comfortable one. It can't all be for Heather's widowhood."

I had told her—we had shared a smile—that often, while we were picking out furniture or rolling on another coat of paint at midnight, I got past a feeling of absurdity that might otherwise have stopped me by telling myself, "Heather needs a nice place." Or: "Let's get this fixed up for her." These variations felt like a pragmatic use of "as if," a kind of self-hypnosis to get the job done.

Dr. George shook her head, looked determined. "I don't believe some part of you is not looking forward to it."

"Maybe there is. It's possible. Some of the time. It's puzzling to me too. Sometimes I feel . . . like I'm trying to stay alive long enough to live."

"Are you sure you're okay to drive?"

☙ In August, shortly before I turned forty-nine, my family announced plans to celebrate my fiftieth birthday at the cottage. Without knowing anything further about the plans, I knew that they would depend on me for their very completion let alone their success. Quietly, diplomatically, I would get the team members up to the event, marshalling the stragglers, harnessing the would-be leaders, healing rifts as they broke open anew; then, if we made it that far, get them—and myself—through the event and beyond it. In my present state, especially, it sounded arduous. It sounded like breaking rocks in the dark.

"The burden of consciousness" was a shorthand phrase Dr. George and I sometimes used, a philosophical truth about the world which states that whoever, in a given situation, is most conscious of what is transpiring will always carry the greatest burden of acting for the others, taking care of them, even, unfair though it may seem, of accepting their responsibility. Caretaking: it falls to the most able. How could it be otherwise? Consciousness imposes costs, though unconsciousness inflicts even sterner ones.

But those who are equipped, by temperament and talents, to assume the job of social caretaking are often the ones who most neglect taking care of themselves. It was this self-caretaking, the awareness and skills necessary for it, that had occupied much of our time in Dr. George's office, and to which we returned now that *leavetaking* had backed off a pace or two. I heard the voice less often now, sometimes only once a day. It was as if the director/playwright had decided he was more satisfied with what was happening onstage, or perhaps he was just biding his time. (There was nothing about that voice that implied it could ever get tired and need a break.) And my grimy ticket taker also glowered less often from his shadows; perhaps he too had other fares to collect.

The metaphors for the cultivation of caretaking, a process that took many forms and was conducted in many moods, involved the mental actions of sifting, sorting, disentangling. Separating was the element common to all these processes. Separating past from present from future (you'll have to pretend you *have* a future for this one, Dr. George joked). Separating oneself from any of the times in one's life: from now, from this moment, even. Separating oneself from others: their lives, their needs. Separating "want" from "deserve" from "will likely get." Separating—this was hard—self from symptom: what may occur from what has occurred, what must always occur. Separating habit from habit: which ones serve and nourish, which ones wear down and destroy. De-routining life. Stopping, or at least slowing, things in their tracks long enough to ask the vital question: Does it need to be this way? Mindfulness (as Dr. George called this process) brought change, subtly but surely. It provided a lever, a pry bar, to insert in a given situation, a fulcrum across which the dead weight of custom might be shifted, budged a crucial inch. And there were smaller, more specific tricks that could help. One I had hit on myself: the pause. Before acting, and especially before answering, if you inserted a shim of time, even a second, there was that much more chance that a self-conscious, participating person would respond instead of an automaton. At the very least, if you still gave the reflex answer you always gave in such an exchange, the instant of reflection would remind you that you were reading from a script. It could make for some comical dead time—a "duh" that perplexed (and that could be wickedly fun)—but it could also mean that you just might have a real conversation.

When it came to being in the world, and viewing oneself in it, Dr. George gave me a mixed review. She praised my insight and perceptiveness when these were focused on others, but she felt that rich outlook became myopic when I considered myself. Friends knew me as a generous person, giving and forgiving, but in my inner life those amplitudes shrivelled, leaving me with a cold, stick-figure scold as *my* companion. It wasn't the whole picture, she hastened to add. That was a big part of what she was trying to say. No mere survival instinct—without a solid measure of self-love—could have carried me through the decades of manias and depressions, at least two psychotic breaks, or pushed me to discover the huge stock of coping strategies—an armamentarium she called it once (we both tried to recall the word and said it at the same time): the dark-room withdrawals, secrecy, alcohol, itinerant jobs, serial addresses, all-night walks. Those were more than symptoms; they were life-wiles too. But—she may even have raised her finger—an overcompensation had occurred. Those coping muscles had been exercised at the expense of the option of improvement; in bodybuilder parlance, maintenance was ripped while thriving atrophied. Or—she switched metaphors as freely as I did sometimes—illness had claimed such a large seat at the table, was so well-fed and corpulent, that any other outlook was impoverished, standing meekly by to take what seconds might be left. Armed as I was against inevitable illness, was I armed also against possible health? Having earned my stripes, unquestioned rank, in one war, could I join another as a foot soldier? She posed a constant question, phrased a hundred ways so I could not evade it. Having grappled with an enemy for low stakes, could I grapple with an ally for higher? When did the habits imposed by sickness become the habits of sickness? Could I learn new habits; could I permit myself that? Or—the subtlest, hardest crux of all—could I forgive myself for the learning already well begun, for the permission already granted? Part of me could: "You're here." The other . . . . ?

Taking tennis lessons, the first thing that goes is your old game. Words from an old psychiatrist, a very urbane and cultured man, though (I see now) too settled in his suavity for the rough-and-tumble that good therapy sometimes requires. We had smiled—there were many smiles in those sessions, though seldom a laugh, and never one from his side—at his description of how his serves, his returns, his volleys had all crumbled under instruction; all the apparatus he had employed for years had broken apart, disintegrated into flails and falls and netted balls, until there was nothing left, and then, step by step, the new strokes could be learned, and with them the new precision and power.

The muscles metaphor brought back another memory too. Once when I was seeing a chiropractor for the first time, his assistant weighed each of my arms in a sling scale as part of the intitial workup. As she wrote down the numbers, she remarked that she had seldom seen someone so "completely left-handed." "But I'm right-handed," I protested, mystified that she would assume otherwise. "That's not possible," she said, then, laughing, admitted that I would know. But, she explained, my left arm had fully thirty percent more muscle mass than my right. Had my right arm been injured? I told her there had been two dislocations in my teens, and since then recurring joint pain that was getting worse with age, sometimes flaring up to the point where I couldn't raise my arm to comb my hair. I tried to keep up the stretching and other exercises in the meantime, I assured her. She nodded yes and shook her head no; she had a way of combining the gestures. Exercise mattered less than daily habits. Which arm do you open doors with? Carry groceries with? Thousands of those kinds of instances, in which one arm was favoured to avoid pain, inevitably weakened the neglected limb. Look at surgery, she said. One day flat on your back and already the muscles have begun to atrophy. Even the couch potato learns how much exercise he was getting inadvertently: walking to the kitchen to fix his snack, hoisting himself out of the chair, crossing the room to insert a video. Pain breeds habits—necessary ones; but carry them on too long, and they breed—? Pain. (The chiropractor was a less charming pedant than his assistant; he turned you into his jointed dummy rather than his stooge, and I quit him soon.) She had given me pause. And now—remembering—pause again.

℞ The poems that would become A *Thaw Foretold* dribbled to a halt in January, a year after I had started them, a year after I had begun seeing Dr. George. I had no other writing projects in mind. That was not unusual, that blank at the end of a spell of work, but this time it felt more final. I felt the Book of Words—or my role of writing in it—coming to a close, ready to be shut, to be fitted back on the shelf. I had always told people—I had said it in a couple of interviews—that I was a reader first and last; the expedition of writing was only a part of that larger exploration. The listeners had looked bemused, but I meant it. Writing as a part of reading, and published writing as a tiny part of writing: one blazed trail in the forest. I had published my first book at forty-one; if all went as scheduled, my sixth would appear just before I turned fifty-one. Six books in ten years: two collections of poems, two collections of short stories, two novels. It had a pleasing symmetry. Cut and print.

Or was that all just tiredness talking—that core weariness in search of the ultimate, the unending nap? *Leavetaking* was back. It had never stopped, but now the frequency stepped up. Apparently it was going to be the soundtrack of 2005—the flat declaration of depletion itself—and it sounded even deader and more slab-naked than before, without the baffling of plans or even many other thoughts, like a remark made in an empty corridor. The ticket taker had worked back around to this end of the platform, too, that patch of muddy gray pushing in from the right.

"The image may be of travel," I told Dr. George, "but the sense I get—I get it all the time now—is of looking for a place to stop. A stopping point, or place."

She raised her eyebrows.

"No, not that. Not in the usual sense anyway." (What other sense was there?) "I just . . . want to stop."

Stop what? Neither of us had to say it aloud.

⊗ Leaving Tim Hortons once after buying a coffee for the drive back to Toronto, I saw a middle-aged man in a wheelchair approaching the double glass doors from the other side.

"I'm okay," he said, opening with one hand the door beside the one I had rushed forward to hold open.

"Are you sure?" I asked.

"Wouldn't I know?"

⊗ Meanwhile there was some work to be done on the book coming out in the fall. Some revisions and correspondence about it, cover ideas and possible photographs, page proofing—each task was welcome, partly as a distraction, but none of them took long enough. Someone would apologize for giving me a deadline of six days, and I would finish the job in six hours. Depletion, I found, could be a black dynamo; it churned out energy even in the absence of sufficient fuel. In fact, the lower the input, the faster the turbine whirred. And I was locating very little input. Even my rock, reading—the one I'd half-bragged was the first and the last—showed signs of crumbling. I would start things and then lay them aside. Fiction, non-fiction, poems, magazines—anything I tried went dusty, blew away. That had happened before, for a few hours, for a bad couple of days—but this stretched on for weeks. (Until finally I found a subject that could hold me, which I will get to shortly.) I despaired at having to learn what the non-readers knew how to do: fill a life devoid of pages. But reading was only the most blatant sign, the leading edge, of a world, mine, turning to the consistency of dry tissue paper, a weightless shredding.

leavetaking

The book I was preparing was called *Catalogue Raisonné*, a title I knew suited the novel pefectly but sometimes regretted choosing because I rarely told it to someone without having to explain what it meant. "A detailed, descriptive inventory of the pieces in an art exhibition," I would hear my voice saying (sometimes over top of *leavetaking*, which often accompanied another track like a film score), "just as the narrator, who is investigating a mystery in an art gallery, is doing a kind of inventory of the pieces of his life. Finding out what's real, what's not. Finding out what's there."

leavetaking

Sometime in April—after some scary drives, 160 km/hr night flights on mental black ice—I hit the break point in Dr. George's office. My game, such as it had become, fell apart in a few moments, so precipitously that I had the physical sensation of dropping through a false floor that I had mistaken for bottom and accelerating toward a true bottom I could not even glimpse yet. "I've hit the wall," I had time to get out, and then the tears were rolling down my face. They came steadily, without sobs or gulps, as if the water in an underground cavern had found these two outlets at my eyes. Dr. George pushed the box of tissues across the table and I used them periodically to keep up with the flow. "I'm at my wit's end," I mumbled. "I can't see a way out." A few other things like that, near the beginning—as if to blur the perfect picture weeping made, or to flee by habit from weeping's total eloquence into some more partial, hence more hopeful, approximation in words. Soon the words fell away; washed away, perhaps. It lasted a long time, perhaps twenty minutes. As my tears slowed I had the certainty, almost restful, that life as I had been living it, not just recently but for a long time, was simply insupportable. Something, many things, had to give. Give way. Change. Would change, one way or another.

Afterward, as I sat there with a ringing head—feeling vanquished but dispensed, dreamily defeated, the way I always imagined a knocked-out boxer might feel coming around on the canvas—Dr. George said quietly, "So, Mike, what are we going to do?"

Her tone ruled out only one option: nothing. From the start she had discussed the possibility of mood-regulating medications, something more focused than the increasing dosages of clonazepam and lorazepam I was getting by on. She thought a newer drug, lamotrigine, was promising; usually it did not involve the cognitive fogging I had found so intolerable with lithium and carbamazepine, and in other ways it matched my profile. Frequently, in our talks, she had suggested it, laying out its strong promise of more stable days; but she never pushed, and always said she understood when I demurred. Now?

"Let's do it," I said.

After we had set things up, Dr. George said, with a sad and caring look, "I don't like to see you suffering so much. I think we can do better."

I nodded. And she added, "Are you okay to drive?"

That day, strangely or not, I was.

ଔ Lamotrigine never got the six-month trial we agreed was needed, however. The side effects I felt as I began to take it were unpleasant but tolerable: some queasiness, blurred vision, dizziness—the vertigo-like package that comes with many of the psychiatric drugs. It had one known side effect that was rare but truly horrifying: exfoliating dermatitis, a potentially fatal sloughing off of the skin, which, to anyone with a visual imagination, conjured a death as a giant chunk of raw and bloody meat, a bipolar Bartholomew flayed by a white tablet. It was extremely rare. But, obviously, serious enough that at the first sign of rash, especially on the lower body, one was to suspend medication and contact the doctor. After a few weeks, when I felt myself adjusting to the drug with fewer ill effects, I was sitting at the desk in my office when Heather, pointing at my thigh, said, "What's that?" I was wearing shorts, and I looked down to see a dark red blotch on my skin, starting at my right knee and extending several inches up my thigh. We thought that perhaps I had pressed my leg against the underside of the desk. But, as we watched, the redness did not diminish; it merely shifted sluggishly from a solid burgundy block to closely spaced dots of bright red, like a crimson sunset by Seurat. I e-mailed Dr. George that I was stopping the drug. Though surprised by the unusual symptom, she agreed that we had no choice but to discontinue the trial.

For once, I had a fallback plan. We had talked at times of some of the promising news about high dosages of omega-3 supplements. Dr. George had found some encouraging and well-designed studies suggesting, at the least, good warrant for further research. It was important, all sources agreed, to find pills of pharmaceutical grade, using molecular distillation, to avoid the potentially high concentrations of mercury and other heavy metals often present in the fish that are the primary source of omega-3 fatty acids. I located the best product I could find (and afford—there were some upscale models) and began my regimen of "fish pills," plus the vitamin E, vitamin C and flaxseed oil that were supposed to enhance the absorption of the omega-3 compounds.

I had just begun this regimen when we went north to my parents' cottage to attend my fiftieth birthday party. Six months later, I am still swallowing my fourteen pills a day, and feeling—cautiously, tentatively—better. There has been no dramatic lift but there has been, perhaps, a levelling off. (Without a damping down, which is the most common trade-off.) From mid-November to now, mid-January, I have worked steadily on these essays, the first time in thirty years I have been productive through December (with one grudging day off for Christmas); for decades, there has been an almost total shutdown for the entire period during which this new writing has taken shape.

But that is to anticipate things—getting ahead of myself in terms of mood and faculties and not only writing again but finding a subject to write about. Last summer I was still swallowing my capsules in the dogged hope of a change rather than from any confirmed sign of one.

ભ Before that, though, by some unknown magic, I hit my reading stride again. I found my subject (or it found me)—it must have been around the time I broke down in Dr. George's office—and in no time I was galloping in it, reading, for a minimum of several hours a day, in a subject I had not given ten minutes thought to in my entire life. The spring, summer and early fall before I started this writing, I read nothing that was not directly connected to the American Civil War. A few items will give a taste of the heaps of war matter I waded through. Carl Sandburg's two-volume biography of Abraham Lincoln, *The Prairie Years* and *The War Years*. Shelby Foote's eight-volume history of the war. Another volume of selected passages by and about Lincoln. Ulysses S. Grant's *Personal Memoirs*. Edmund Wilson's *Patriotic Gore*, which examines the conflict through the writings produced before, during and after it. Studying old maps and reading first-hand accounts, I came to know the course and depths of streams, the weather of one hundred and forty years ago, the elevation of bluffs and the types of trees found in a forest (as well as the number of bullets extracted from one of those trees after a battle), in places, some of which I had never heard of before and others I knew only as classroom names, yet which now seemed more real to me than the Toronto street I lived on or the apartment I was sitting in. Harper's Ferry, Manasses (First and Second), Fort Henry and Fort Donelson, Shiloh, Vicksburg, Chancellorsville, Perrysville, Gettysburg . . . the list could go on down this page and the next, from siege to battle to skirmish to sniper fire at a crossroads. Where had this sudden obsession come from? Previously I had felt only a passing interest in the convulsion to the south. Yes, I was born in Rochester, Minnesota, to Canadian parents, but I spent only the first two years of my life there, have no memories of it, and have lived in Canada for the succeeding forty-eight years. Yet it was not just passionate interest I felt in the subject, but also a dispassionate comfort I took from immersing myself in it. It felt like coming home. After watching Ken Burns's eleven-hour documentary on the war, I went back and watched it all again and some episodes many times. I hummed parts of the movie's score and the period songs used in it. When reading, I held books an inch from my face to study the astonishingly clear and detailed photographs of Sherman, Lee, Grant, Lincoln, Halleck, McClellan, Johnston, Beauregard, Forrest . . . and scores of ordinary soldiers and slaves and men and women. Lincoln's long, seamed face often appeared vividly before me, both in dreams and when I was awake, a forceful vision just this side of hallucination. Sometimes the force of that gaze lifted me right out of sleep, clear awake and staring about the room. Then, as soon as I began the first of the entries that would go toward this book, I set down my Civil War material and have not picked it up since. My bookmark is right where I left it in *The Lincoln Reader*.

A specimen of Lincoln's thought, and my half-year obsession, survives in a quotation that I printed on a cardboard square and inserted, and still keep, in my wallet. It is from the President's message to Congress, delivered on December 1, 1862: "As our case is new, so must we think anew, and act anew. We must disenthrall ourselves."

(On the other side of the cardboard square, a fitting · accidental bedfellow, is Updike's poignant tribute to Melville: "In his professional defeat his imagination remained his own.")

CR After the summer, my diet of fish pills and other supplements firmly in place, I started to feel a bit better. There was an incremental lightening, as if a worker were unloading, one brick at a time, the stacks on a pallet I was lying under. There was still no writing, nor thoughts of any—not for eight months now. That felt strange: sedate, non-urgent—it would take some getting used to. I still had my Civil War reading, and my day job of tutoring had started up again after Labour Day. It was a full-time schedule, but without the second job of writing crammed before and after it (even, at the most hectic times, into the spare half minutes during it), I felt like a retiree. New spaces yawned around me.

I heard *leavetaking* less often. It too seemed to be taking a breather, which perplexed me a little. The director could not be content with the direction this production was taking—could he? My ticket taker, except for occasional gray sidlings at my elbow, had wandered off too. As the end-of-October launch date for the novel approached, a flurry of proofing and correspondence simulated the act of writing, and I was energized by it. Of course, the advent of a new book, the publisher's hopes for it, my flutterings of hope for it—this called on future-thinking, the kind I was no good at, except by resorting to the "as if" strategies I had worked out with Dr. George. Still, I carried off the launch, a reading at a literary festival and a book club meeting (all but one event in this book's short public run) with an almost suspicious lack of serious nerves. Aplomb? Apathy? They could mimic each other, I knew.

"No sign of my evil twin," I reported to Dr. George after one of these outings. "Or, no, he was there. He just didn't have that much to say. He started up at times . . . but never got too out of hand."

"The evil twin. Is that what we're calling your ticket taker now?"

"He is the same person, I think. Just the speaking version. The one with the soundtrack on permanent repeat:

You suck. You're sick. No future. They despise you. They should. You . . . et cetera."

Dr. George remained silent a few moments, as if she was piecing something out. "But the evil twin puts the ticket taker in another light, doesn't he?"

"How?"

Well, she explained, what is a twin after all? Someone who is as close as one person can be to another, but is still a separate—a separable—individual. The awareness of an enemy, a menacing other—and the illness certainly could be considered that, she agreed—was at least one vital step away from having that adversary as an indistinguishable part of yourself, a self-countering part of your everyday makeup.

"Isn't it possible," she said, "that although you're together at the station, you're not going to take the trip together? He's importunate—insistent, you called him—because he knows you're leaving him behind."

"No room."

"No room. No time. How about no need?"

"He could be the one going, while I stay behind."

"Maybe he's asking you for the fare so he *can* go."

"*Hasta la vista.* Don't forget to write."

CR   The endgame came in November, as so many of my endgames had. Those terminations had often been dire: self-mutilation, admission to hospital; suicide attempts; suicide plans—and at the best of times had been stalemates: long lying-ins in a dark or one-lamped room, waiting to be delivered back to functioning. Initial harbingers suggested that this November might yet turn out like those.

On November 10, toting boxes of books, I returned to my alma mater, McMaster University, to give a talk on my

127

life and writing. I had earned my B.A. on the "eleven year plan," as I joked at one point in my talk; the reasons for the interruptions I was not quite prepared to confide to strangers. Arts Matter, the student group that had invited me, left me free to discuss whatever I wanted, but asked that it run to about an hour, with a question and answer period to follow. "The Missing Chord" (the phrase came from *Catalogue Raisonné*)—which took three days to prepare and fifty minutes to deliver—was ambitious, perhaps overly so, including excerpts from all five books and suggesting the delicate and mysterious tendrils spiralling between them and my actual life, using metaphors that ranged among botany (root and flower), astronomy (black holes, event horizons), geometry (tangents to circles), and magnetism (iron filings jumping into patterns as a magnet passes beneath the surface they lie on). It seemed to go all right. One listener was rapt; three were attentive; one yawned; one slept. I was glad it went at all. Twenty minutes after the advertised 7:00 p.m. start, only the three members of Arts Matter stood beside me and my stacks of books. Wait another five minutes, I advised; my mom had said she would come. And she did, eventually finding the room on the seventh floor of Togo Salmon Hall. Two more minutes, I said; two friends from Toronto had said they would drop by on their way to dinner with their daughter. When they arrived, I made my last suggestion: pull six chairs close around mine; if it could not be large, let it at least be intimate. For six as for sixty (though I have never faced half that many), I threw myself into it. Questions were asked; four books were bought. We put the chairs back precisely in the positions we had found them, the stipulation most emphasized by the university.

My feeling afterward was of utter depletion more than failure. My hands shook like aspen leaves when I raised them from the steering wheel (I wasn't okay to drive). What is this? I thought. This cored, drained state—this rapid coring and draining at any event, whether private or public, successful or unsuccessful. Was it really the exhaustion of swimming continuously upstream—or feeling that I was—quivering like a salmon that has navigated a series of difficult channels, almost dried up in places and in others choked with debris, and has cleared, sometimes after innumerable attempts, downstream waterfalls, only to find itself at last confronted by the towering wall of a concrete dam, up a fraction of which it is manifestly impossible to leap but against which it must nevertheless repeatedly throw itself? Melodramatic the image might be, self-pitying, but it felt right. It was not that there had not been successes, but these had been personal, sometimes Pyrrhic victories, times when I knew I had acquitted myself well against steep odds. What was I looking for—an *impersonal* victory? In a way, perhaps. A victory where you felt yourself meshing with events, not merely subduing them; a win where the world met you halfway.

The next morning, after a few hours sleep, I was on the same highway driving back to Hamilton for my appointment with Dr. George. On the way, I toyed with the outline of a little story, which could be written as a story or just sketched as the idea for one, the way Kurt Vonnegut had often included synopses of Kilgore Trout's stories in his novels. In my tale of consensual cannibalism—"The Rending," "The Reading," "The Rendition"—I am staked out on a low table, face to fluorescent lights, speaking from inside a well of my own reverberating voice as the six begin to eat me painlessly—with tickling, occasionally throbbing, nibbles and bites—starting from my two hands, two legs, the top of the head, the lower abdomen. I lose the power to move, then to see, smell, hear—finally, to speak. There remains only my beating heart, or an ache in the centre of me where a heart used to beat—which "owing to Great Aunt Elena's delicacy of feeding or the deteriorating condition of her teeth, persists in its tremulous convulsions long after all other motion and sense have ceased."

I had once told Dr. George that I had a feeling of having gone on for a long while on pure heart. Her eyes said: Not enough.

Lost in thought in the waiting room, I caught a phrase from a nearby radio: "The Seventh Book of Remembrance." What was that, a line from Revelation? In any case, it had a nice, allusive ring. Then I heard trumpet notes, and turned and saw Anna M. standing there, looking near me if not quite at me. Anna, who is employed in some capacity upstairs, has never given any sign of recognizing me when she has passed (nor have I ever given her such a sign), although twenty years ago she was a close friend of the woman I lived with then and was often over at our apartment, usually to talk about the man she was dating. In small doses I had found her charming, a petite dark flirt, silly but sparkly; I had one strong memory of her listing, from within a voluminous fur coat, all the boxes on her "perfect man" checklist: between this age and that, with at least this much income, minimum height, maximum weight—we had laughed and argued, drinking wine. Now she looked worn, haggard, stern. It was as if the oblivious young flirt had passed to censorious matron seamlessly. Was that why she pretended not to know me? And did I too look that used-up, that almost-unplaceable?

"Hello," I said this time, since she was standing so close. Giving no sign of having heard me, she bent to the radio on the low table between us and turned the volume up.

The trumpet verged on piercing. Only then—Christ, how out of it can you be? I thought—did I remember that it was 11:00 a.m. on Remembrance Day. On this day, almost at this hour, twenty-eight years ago I had first been admitted to hospital as a psychiatric patient: a symbolism too portentous ever to fly in fiction. The closest I had come were my years of notes and outlines for *11:11*—a projected novel of the afterlife or, more precisely, of a character who may or may not be dead, who cannot determine that or, if he is dead, how he should operate in the new realm, what rules and procedures apply. I turned my head to stare into unfocused space, then shut my eyes while the trumpet gave way to silence, a silence observed upstairs and downstairs in the old house, no machines clicking, no footsteps overhead—as if the world had indeed stopped to remember. I felt the deep satisfaction and peace of the stopping point, the stoppage and the silence, into which memory may flow more readily but so may many other things . . . so may anything. So refreshing, so sane, so solid. And then the trumpet again.

Thumbing through a *Sports Illustrated* magazine—my thoughts drifting as I took in the bright colours and determined faces of football players, golfers, cyclists—I thought of my brother Greg, my younger look-alike, hale and handsome, with his black dog, Ebony. An athlete was posed with his dog in the playroom of his mansion, a picture not of solitary hunting in shadowy woods but of its opposite, of conspicuous enjoyment of one's achievement in society, of the sunlit self in repose.

Dr. George opened her door and I took my seat at her round wooden table. As I began speaking about the talk the night before, I could feel an answer mingled in my words, dissolved in them, like salt in water. I described how absorbed I had felt writing the drafts of my talk, how I had dreaded the chore but then got swept up in it. Now, I said, becoming excited as I thought of it, I wanted to try to turn the talk into an autobiographical essay. I had not written an essay since my last year of university and I had never written anything explicitly autobiographical. The thought of doing such work had always filled me with ennui. Now there was nothing else I wanted to do. The urge invaded and occupied me fully, like my Civil War reading, which was over now. Beyond this essay, I bubbled at Dr. George, I was resolved to embark on a discovery of *leavetaking*, of the word's possibilities. "What else have you been doing, right?" she said. Yes: I looked at her: Yes! The topic had been in front of us all these months; with Dr. George's help, I had been working on it without pause. To what else had I devoted even a fraction of the same intensity, the same concentration? Recognizing this came with a feeling of being stung awake, as by a good hard slap, and of solidity, as if a square peg I had been trying to wrestle into various round holes had finally found the four-cornered, right-sized niche that had been waiting for it. It felt like the climax of one of those old-fashioned mystery dramas where the murder weapon—in this case the writing weapon, the subject—is discovered to have been under the sleuth's nose all the time. You had to follow all the false trails to get backed into this last, right corner.

Leavetaking. I realized I had not heard it in days.

ଔ   A snowstorm, then the Christmas holidays, put off my next meeting with Dr. George until early January, almost exactly two years after we had begun. By that time, working every day—with just the one reluctant stop for Christmas dinner—I had completed drafts of the first two of these essays. How did it feel? Dr. George wanted to know. It felt harrowing, very dark to revisit some places, haunted zones—but (I had to consider this carefully) perhaps not more harrowing or difficult than other writing had been. It was time: I had enough distance from the subject, seemingly, though where that distance had come from was a mystery; somehow, though, there was the necessary sliver of space between my skin and what I was stitching. Also—and this was an enormous help on any project—there was nothing I was even remotely as interested in doing. I had not seen it coming, but I was ready . . . ripe.

All that was left was the last essay. "Leavetaking," of course.

"Do you have any sense how that one will go?"

I had the usual premonitions. Vague contours. A sense of the parameters. The desiderata and the possible pitfalls. "And I know how it will end." I had found an image that summed up *leavetaking* for me, without explaining it exactly, and even as I began uncertainly to write this, I knew that it would have to be the final image. It fit—for reasons I could not yet articulate.

"So you have a stop."

"A start."

"Don't they always come as a pair?"

There was a giddy sense in the room that day. We had had fun in our meetings before—our senses of humor were compatible and had blended to give us frequent breaks from the heavier going—but on this day it was as if we had signed a pact to suspend all slogging, to just revel in an hour of comradely talk. I described the two essays I had written and said I had been changing my mind about their order. "Two Rooms," though I had written it first, had originally figured in the middle, I thought, or even at the end, a climax. But now I saw it coming first; I had that instinct about it, growing stronger, without knowing why I felt that way. I quoted the first line: "How much of our lives happens while we are unconscious?" (I had already described the essay's depiction of electroshock and a near drug overdose.)

"That makes sense then," said Dr. George. "It's the movement from unconsciousness . . . passive suffering—"

"To conscious, active suffering!"

I laughed; Dr. George merely smiled.

"There's a world of difference, isn't there?"

"Yes," I admitted. And, later, thought: That's exactly the difference there is: A world.

ও In July, on a day of baking heat, Heather and I had driven over to Hamilton in search of a possible cover photograph for *Catalogue Raisonné*. We wanted to shoot the Skyway Bridge, which plays a small but important part—in the form of someone's fatal drop—in the novel. First we stopped on the Burlington side of the beach strip. It had been twenty or thirty years since I had visited the east end of the city. Walking along the shore, among sunbathers and splashing children, the first thing that struck us, in this industrial zone notorious for its pollution, was the beauty. The sand was white and floury; the water, undergoing treatments and said to be improving, looked blue and sparkling. We sat down on a huge bleached log under some shade-giving maples; sighting through a rectangle framed by lush foliage, a white sailboat cutting across sapphire water, we remarked on how the scene could pass for a snapshot from a Caribbean holiday. Of course, that was facing out into Lake Ontario, but the inner harbor, for years a cesspool, the butt of Hammer jokes, a public shame, the price of steel—offered similar surprises. At the end of a long concrete pier, two men were fishing for perch. Perch, that clean-living fish, in a sludge pond that supposedly had been deserted by all but the giant carp, deformed by poisons, stirring up more silts with their bottom feeding. As if on cue, one of the fisherman hooked a perch and reeled it in. It had to be toxic, cancered—the steel companies with their flames and smoke were right across the bay—but it looked a healthy specimen. Plump white belly, bright orange fins, dark stripes. He dropped it flopping in a pail with several others. Was he actually going to eat it? We took some good shots of the bridge, from underneath, looking up at its side-by-side double rows of concrete support pillars, the twin lanes far above, the complex steel beams of the superstructure. From down here it did not look as high as I remembered, though I knew that it was high enough to do its job in the novel.

Under the bridge was more the kind of terrain I had expected: mangy, beige-gray, almost colourless grass, worn away to dirt where cars had parked and roared after hours; scattered bottles and other litter (though not the condoms we expected). We roamed around that dingy nowhere zone, a poster-ready patch of industrial wasteland. The cars droned overhead. The steel companies clanked and smoked across the water. We were about to leave, when a mallard hen veered straight out from the bleak grass, not three feet in front of us, and went quacking loudly over the water. We jumped back, startled; I had felt the gusts of air from her wingbeats. A nesting duck? Here? Heather stayed back on the dirt path where we had been walking, but I, though I was afraid to disturb the nest, could not resist taking a look. Greg had told me how cunningly they could be hidden—he had counted eggs on one summer job—so I was prepared to look and look before I caught the gleam of shell. I was counting on it in fact. I had seen exactly where she had got up from, and I walked in pinsteps slowly back and forth over the area, inching my way along for fear of crushing the eggs.

But I saw no sign of the nest, though I walked a criss-cross grid in the two square meters or so she *must* have come from, peering at the ground, bending as low as arthritic knees would allow. No sign: just the stubby pale grasses, scraggy weeds . . . cracked dirt, scuffed smooth in places. No matter how hard I looked, it remained invisible, what she had been guarding. I gave up finally and walked back to the dirt track, though I am sure I persisted longer than a less curious person might have done.

The Lily Pond

A frog sits on a lily pad near the middle of the pond. He sits so still, so motionless, he might be a ceramic frog on the green, glazed lid of a casserole. What is cooking in the pond under this lid? In the frog's best future, he will never find out. Though he is curious all the same, spurred on by the same restlessness that brought him, by a series of precisely delicate hops, from lily pad to lily pad, out to where he crouches now. Perils surround him: in the water, fish and snapping turtles; in the air, hawks, ospreys, crows, and gulls; on land, snakes and herons and raccoons and frogs only slightly larger than himself, who, like him, will attempt to swallow anything moving that will fit into their mouths. But for now he is safe, warming his blood in the sun, absorbing a film of moisture through his skin. His lily pad, his platform, is a reprieve. All he really has in his favour is his protective colouring, his stillness, and, when all else fails, his jumping —the prodigious, predator-perplexing leaps for which his lightness and long muscles, his fused bones and sliding pelvis, his shock-absorbing joints have prepared him over a quarter of a billion years.

Colour. Stillness. Leaping. It seems a small bag of tactics to pit against the teeming devils of the pond.

Yet it is what he has, what he knows.

For now, it is enough.

છ "There's a pair of us," Heather says to me, a bit breathlessly, after we have left the psychiatrist's office and are sitting in our car. It is early June. She has turned in her seat to face me, and her eyes are wide and lambent, glittering with that desperate euphoria, or euphoric desperation, that has lit them—except when they have gone overcast, shrouded in cancelling gloom—for these last few burning, tumultuous weeks.

She seems relieved for the moment. To have a diagnosis, an illness with a name? (She had feared having a name, but then feared more being something unnamable.) To be sharing, as we have shared so much, a diagnosis with me? "It always amazes me how often you people find each other," the psychiatrist remarked, when I had joined them in the office for the last ten minutes of Heather's interview. He spoke of the number of "bipolar couples" he had met, who had been drawn irresistibly together (often despite existing marriages or other serious obstacles) and who had established unusual but sustaining ways of coping with their cycles of illness, often long before either of them had been diagnosed. Heather and I exchange a look. His bemused, somewhat clinical reflections make it sound as if he is describing a species of exotic animals, creatures that emit a special mating call, inaudible or registered as noise outside their kind, and then embark on bizarre and esoteric mating rites. Yet the gist of his remarks rings true. From the start, Heather and I have been able to speak in shorthand, with intuitive understanding, of steeply swinging moods and strange mental states, and we quickly developed ways of gearing together discordant swings and of warily surviving the most dangerous times, when the swings coincide and amplify each other. We have even joked of a day like today, when Heather's distrust of doctors would relent (gently, in our fantasy, not under the duress of crisis) and we would "make it official."

But the day foreseen is not the day that arrives. I look through the windshield up the street, which is lined with parked cars and empty of people. The leaves of the overhanging shade trees are a bright, incongruous green; we have been keeping such wildly irregular hours lately that it has been a long time since I have paid attention to such basics as the weather or the changing season.

It is Sunday morning, early, before church even. It seems a strange time to be meeting with a psychiatrist outside of an emergency ward, but this psychiatrist has a quirky schedule and neither of Heather's other two doctors felt that it was safe to wait another day. The appointment was scheduled by telephone late last night. This recognition of the need for haste, of the peril Heather is in despite her equable demeanor, inclines me to trust these doctors, despite my own long history of damage by medical misadventure. Already they understand Heather well enough to know that she, like me, will understate rather than exaggerate a crisis, and understate with a more savage discretion as the crisis nears its climax. Suicide, for such a person, does not come as the final escalation of a series of prior warnings and attempts; it comes as a quietly decided act, the click of a turned lock after the guests have gone and the party room has been tidied.

Is it time yet? The question, sceptical but insistent —shadowing the mind at dawn, at noon, at 2:00 a.m.—has altered to a more drastic shape: *Is there still time?* Out of the myriad confusions of the last few harrowing weeks, Heather and I have arrived at one certainty: medical intervention is required. To wait, to hope for change, is no

139

longer permissible; it is not safe. In this, at least, the doctors and we are in accord.

As we drive off toward the pharmacy where we will fill Heather's first prescription of lithium, she murmurs again, softly, as if to herself, "a pair of us." Thinking of the Emily Dickinson poem she is quoting from, in which one frog discourses to another, I wonder if I am hearing, besides a mixed and quizzical expression of relief, a first sign of the controlling image of Heather's sickness—or, could it be, the hopeful image of her health? For if you find yourself floundering between elemental extremes, might not the image of an amphibian be a comfort, a guide? As precarious as a frog's survival may be, as it undoubtedly *is*, it has to afford more hope than the dominant image shaped by, and then shaping, my own first psychosis. Through the summer and fall of 1977, I kept seeing, faintly and intermittently at first, and then constantly and with bullying vividness, a seam of red glowing from within a brownish crust—like molten lava glowing under soil or rock, presaging volcanic eruption. The image was pregnant with violence, a fiery birth that I saw approaching and desired as a consummation, and it ended with blood spilling down my abdomen from the "self-Caesarean" I had performed on myself.

Twenty-nine years later, my thoughts are focused, as they have been for weeks, on how Heather might be spared such a moment, along with its lifelong ramifications, its endlessly rippling aftermath. Surely, I think, my own huge kit bag of mental illness must contain a few instruments to help another. Diet, daily habits, even lighting and room layouts—what might be changed? What might be tinkered with? The smallest adjustment could make a difference, tip the balance. And to that end, everything—even the grotesque, 4:00 a.m. arguments our sleepless, cross-wired selves inveigle us into—must be examined (in retrospect in those cases) for a possible clue.

As I drive down the surreally bright, surreally empty streets, I try to remember the exact wording of the Dickinson poem. Beside me, Heather is slumped in her seat; she is staring blankly ahead. I imagine the glum routines of drug therapy—*on my way to fill my scrip*—pressing in on her.

> *I'm Nobody! Who are you?*
> *Are you—Nobody—Too?*
> *Then there's a pair of us?*
> *Don't tell! they'd advertise—you know!*

The poet's frog is all questions, exclamations, and commands. There's not a single croak of reasoned calm amid the flurry of agitated queries and exhortations. It sounds familiar, which means it is not what I am looking for. The last line in the stanza, in particular, is almost exactly the answer Heather has given me when I have suggested, and at times urged more forcefully, that she should inform those close to her about what is happening. "You don't have to run an ad," I say. "Pick your shots. Only tell someone if it would make your communication too tortuous, too evasive and unreal, not to tell them." As yet, Heather isn't buying it.

Dickinson's question mark—*Then there's a pair of us?* —isn't helpful either. I am glad Heather forgot or ignored it. Sometimes I imagine a flint-eyed observer watching the two of us and thinking, The blind leading the blind. Someone with my record, trying to help someone in Heather's situation—Who worse? I imagine them thinking.

On the other hand: Who better?

CR "Why won't this end?" was the question I kept asking Dr. George during the winter and early spring of 2006. "Why won't this finish? Why is it still hanging on?" However I phrased it, the question was not, as it had been so often before, about mental illness or my life as interwined with it; this time, it was about the three autobiographical essays I had just finished writing, which I had collectively entitled *Leavetaking*. I had cleaned up the manuscript to a readable state, polished it as best I could for now, and had copied and given it to five readers including Dr. George. Aside from a certain anxiety about what the responses would be, I felt the project was finished. It had drained me, emptied the well right down to dry stone. Not only did I have no further desire to work on it, but I felt that further writing down the line, of any kind, would be preposterous. This blankness, a vacancy so thorough it was as if my insides had been sucked out by a shop vacuum, was familiar; it signalled completion of something important, and was endurable as such. But the blankness itself was different this time: not the inert, slow-blinking heaviness, the mindless gape; this was an anxious blankness, a tenterhooks suspension, as if I had produced an egg, with no idea of its ultimate contents, and was waiting for it to hatch.

What was missing most, I told Dr. George, was a sense of the project receding, the almost physical sense of the finished writing taking a step away from me, an inch at first, then another, then a good firm stride. By such steps the work went out there, in the world, on its own—even if "out there" was only as far, physically, as a binder in my bookcase. *Leavetaking*, though, was hovering. It was right beside me, breathing down my neck.

We questioned the usual suspects. (The persistence of *Leavetaking*, ironic given its title, came up in every session through February and March and on into April; no matter where we entered the maze of therapy or what passageways we tried, at some point we would round a corner and find it waiting for us.) Was I worried about the readers' reactions? In a personal sense, not terribly: the small circle of people I had chosen either knew my story well already or were important enough to me that I wanted them to know it better. And in a literary sense, even less so perhaps: I knew the essays were good, they had depth and resonance; I would be disappointed, not shattered, if someone couldn't see that. Besides, one of my five, a writer friend, had phoned right back suggesting places I might submit the individual essays; another, the editor of four of my books, had written asking me to consider publishing them with him. Was that it then? Fear of such a personal story *being* published, read by strangers? No—that, if it happened at all, was a long way off. I had no such plans at the moment. *That* felt new. Having the confidence in something not to nail-bite it forward, but rather to let its future unfold.

None of those normal anxieties was sufficient to explain the sense I had of *Leavetaking* hovering near me, the oppressive but at times strangely comforting claustrophobia produced by its closeness. Its imminence. Or even—in the sense of all-pervasiveness—its immanence.

"It's just . . . *there*," I said one time, exasperated. "*Here*. All the time. It doesn't move. It doesn't budge an inch."

"Because you're still living it," said Dr. George. She may have shrugged slightly.

Real-life narratives were "unfinalizable," she said, but then used an adverb that seemed to contradict that point.

"It isn't finished yet," she said.

By mid-April or so, Heather was in serious trouble. She was in deep water before either of us quite realized she had left the bank. (It is early September now, and Heather has resumed working on her art, which had stumbled to a complete stop during the summer. A picture from the early spring, which she is still elaborating, is a large pencil drawing of Ophelia, buoyed up by her billowing dress and lit by a cold moon, floating, or sinking slowly, in dark rippled water on which, here and there, isolated patches of lily pads cluster.) Even if I could tell Heather's story, her real story, from the inside—which is impossible, both because it is hers and because it is still unfolding—I would not be able to say when this particular episode began. Heather isn't sure herself. What seemed familiar—depression, anxiety, a not-myself unease—accelerated and distorted until they did not resemble, except by analogy, anything she had experienced previously. A change not only quantitative but qualitative had occurred . . . was—is still—occurring.

These things begin with such branching subtlety, twining tendrils of the new around old roots and branches, that there is no way to pinpoint their origins—not at the time, and not even in retrospect. Not until the process is sufficiently underway do you spot an outgrowth, a flower—a symptom. And deepening the confusion is the fact that what is new seems like a thing—*not me, not my life*—and yet it is a thing that can only grow and express itself through a life, mingling inextricably with it. You may feel that something is subverting your will, betraying it—and something may in fact be doing so, if what you mean by your self is your self-in-health—but if so, the invader can only work by annexing your will, working *through* your will. It is a stealth attack, to which most of the incestuous terminology of modern warfare applies: diplomatic maneuverings, pressure points, secret cells, covert agents, sleeper agents, terror tactics, pro-paganda, appeasement; most importantly, resistance *and* col-laboration.

The plant was already well-rooted and flourishing, the campaign well-advanced on many fronts, by the time Heather's typical day encompassed working a full shift in the framing department, closing a bar with friends, and then, glitter-eyed and exhaling alcohol, setting up her laptop or ea-sel to work in the four hours she had until the alarm rang for her morning shift.

Already far along by the time I looked into her eyes and saw, for the first time in fifteen years, someone—some-thing—I did not recognize.

She spoke in those early (but already late) days of what she was "carrying . . . dragging with me." Flipping through a book on Siamese twins at the time, I was struck by the pa-thetic detail of one conjoined twin carrying his dead sibling around until the poisons from his decay contaminated him and he succumbed; and by the even more gruesome ac-counts of those with faces on their chests or the backs of their heads, other flesh-masks drooling, gibbering, weeping or smiling, on their own time, for their own "reasons."

Later, when Heather had collected the books on am-phibians that fascinated and rested her, especially late at night, she saw, and we examined together, pictures that seemed to enlarge the metaphors of development, from seed to maturity, from first contact to "stepping away," that I had discussed with Dr. George. Dr. George, a mother of two, agreed that the parent/child relationship provided a useful, if limited, analogy for artistic as well as other forms of creation: the seed of conception, a byproduct, unnoticed and unno-ticeable at first; the first stirrings of a new complexity within, along with nausea or euphoria, or both, individualized reckonings with the invader; the nudges and swellings of growth; absorption, the filling out, which demands a certain narcissism, a willed blindness to the world . . . and so on, up to the ordeal of delivery . . . and then, though all is present as potential, the endless shepherding of the newcomer through all the tottering, tear-fogged stages that must be surmounted if the thing alive is ever to become a mature individual . . . all of these infinite steps and processes undertaken, yes, so that one day—the sum of many days, many moments—the coddled one can step away as an intimately connected but independent entity, an other.

Except that all of that's too normal for us now. Too pink and blue and stork-delivered. Now, when Heather feels herself crumbling and reconfiguring inside, we need birth from a slant, births in a funhouse mirror. So, opening any of the dozen books on amphibians that surround the bed, we goggle at pictures of frog amplexus, the awkward-looking embraces that frogs maintain so that sperm and eggs may be expelled and fertilized outside the body, a kind of slimy halo of conception in which the partners huddle and grip. Many strategies of amplexus have evolved to help the slippery, short-armed breeders achieve and maintain the necessary proximity. Inguinal, axillary, cephalic, straddle amplexus. Glued amplexus, in which the male secretes a sticky substance to attach himself to the female's back; only after egg-laying will the substance break down, or the female shed her skin, allowing them to go their separate ways. Prolonged amplexus is just what it says: the breeding pair stays locked together for several days or even weeks, the female lugging her mate around as she feeds, the male on top, unable to feed well or at all, becoming thinner and thinner. I remind Heather of her *I'm carrying something . . . dragging something.* "Me?" I say. She chuckles.

And that—moments of lightness when we carry on as we always have—is one of the supernally weird features of this thing. (All right, this illness—though I have advised Heather to treat her diagnosis as a working hypothesis, no more, no less; neither to be embraced docilely nor spurned defiantly (extremes I know are dangerous), but to be considered for just as long as it seems to jibe with experience and offer the possibility of easement. Not a second more, I emphasize; but Heather isn't really listening. That Sunday morning in the car—a few days back but seeming months distant—the diagnosis might have been a tag to cling to, but now she is down in the muck, in amplexus with the thing—swallowing three drugs, seeing three doctors—debating with me nightly whether she can continue working, whether she should be hospitalized—and she has to wonder when, and how, a name becomes a role . . . a verdict. A sentence?)

And still, and yet, these strange, still moments of dispensation. So surreal, so welcome. Comforting, disquieting. The house is being battered by a hurricane and we are serving tea as usual in the drawing room.

෯ 4:14 a.m. Now she has flipped past amplexus into egg- and tadpole-carrying. Not the sensible amphibians who lay the eggs in water and hop away, leaving them to their fate; Heather has found the bizarrely burdened ones, who lug their fecundity around with them. The male midwife toad, carrying strings of fertilized eggs wrapped around his hind legs for up to a month, releasing the tadpoles only when they are ready to hatch. And, oddest of the tadpole-carrying parents, Darwin's frog, *Rhinoderma darwini*, the male of which hovers near the eggs until the tadpoles begin to squirm in the jelly, then picks them up in his mouth; when they are fully

147

developed, after about three weeks, he spits them out. Or this—I lean over to see a female *Rheobatrachus silus*, from Australia, who somehow broods her young in her stomach, which distends into a sac-like organ taking up most of her body cavity, its powerful digestive juices switched off by a chemical secreted by the tadpoles, which, after they are fully formed, are ejected from their mother's mouth. What might the Goya of *Saturn Devouring His Children* do with *that*? On my side of the bed, along with more amphibian lore, I have *Inside Hitler's Bunker*, a recent account by the German historian Joachim Fest. I return to that grotesquerie with no sense of disjunction. Our alarm will ring in less than three hours.

෬ Soon these near-all-nighters come to an end. Lamotrigine has been added to the lithium, which makes three drugs counting the antidepressant she started with and still takes, with a threefold increase in the dosages of all three. Mania has been bludgeoned still, a mere rolling and flicking behind mostly closed eyelids. After dragging herself groggily through her day ("making many mistakes . . . not thinking," she mutters, and sometimes weeps quietly over), she falls asleep suddenly, snatched from consciousness the way Persephone is yanked underground by Pluto in the woodcut Heather is carving (carving now, in September, when she has resumed art, not in the zombie-like early summer I am describing): the God of the Dead a bald and blank-faced muscleman, Pharaonic-looking in his kilt and heavy, twisted torso; the naked girl's arms and legs and hair flying straight out ahead of her from the sheer velocity of her abduction; the daylight already far above, a round diffused glimmer as from a flashlight shone into a hole.

Lying on her back, the bedside light still on, she is already breathing heavily and slowly, already deep into the five-fathoms sleep of the drugged. Her parted lips exhale a faint, musty-metallic odor that is alien yet familiar.

Gently—though she is past the stage of stirring—I remove the book lying open across her middle, her hands placed palms down on it. She had time to open it to just one page, one image to take with her down into sleep, and I stare at what she was seeing.

Paradox Frogs, *Pseudis paradoxa*, of South America. Massive, bloated brown tadpoles (shown), whose adult form (not shown) was only recently "discovered," since it is a small frog of normal slimness, just one fourth the size of its larval state. Biologists had not seen it because they had been looking on the wrong scale. This strange creature fits, bizarrely, with the description I have just been reading of Hitler's eleventh-hour wedding to Eva Braun in the bunker. Previously wedded only to an abstract and fantastic History, pledged in this realm to monomaniacal bachelorhood, Hitler, when he decides for whatever reasons to take an earthly bride, becomes, in the familiar and banal ritual described —signing the register, the flustered bride crossing out the "B" she started to write and correcting it to her new name; the toasts at the shabby reception—almost shockingly familiar. In this homely social ceremony Hitler seems more recognizably human, as he does in his bunker depressions and tirades, the world-tyrant screaming from the more usual confines of a cage. With the legs of the paradox frog, thought takes a paradox leap: Could megalomania be a larval state of the soul? Hitler as half-born, slow-born, passing through a monstrous and inhuman adolescence as a genocidal dictator to become his adult self, a shrunken and infirm old psychopath dying in a bunker, pathetic and frightening in his self-pity and paranoia, his boundless loathing, but also, finally, long too late, recognizably a sick human. His gestation was protracted and external to the womb, and it became the world's nightmare. Otherwise—what? A career as a more local sicko and oppressor—a gang leader? A serial killer? A deadly, but infinitely smaller, adult.

At a catch in Heather's breathing, I turn anxiously and the bubble of distraction pops. Hitler the paradox frog hops crazily away. I realize that I have been using these abstruse reflections mainly as a way to make the time pass. Help the seconds tick by, past this time when Heather is still so sick, to a time when she may be well again.

"You're not sick. You're worried sick," Dr. George said recently.

She's right. All through the time of Heather's sickness, including the weeks when I sensed it but could not admit it consciously, acids have been churning in my stomach, tension knotting my muscles from my neck down to my calves . . . yet I have felt sane. Because I've needed to be?

"She's phenomenally lucky to have you at this time," Dr. George said in another meeting. And I cringed at that—partly because, for all my thirty-year experience with this illness, I feel helpless so often, unable to know what is happening, after all, deep inside Heather, and so unable to do more (though I hope this may be much) than offer comfort and support while the process unfolds; and partly, too, I cringed because of the very intensity with which I do hope that my decades of fighting this thing—my version of it anyway—might prove valuable. Might even prove, in my fondest fantasy, a treasure trove. Is that just vanity, wanting to see my own wasted years turn to some positive account? "The Madman Sage" instead of "The Frog Prince?" "'T'were to consider the thing too curiously," murmurs my inner Horatio.

I *want* Heather to be phenomenally lucky. I want it day and night. I want her to thrive.

First, though, she has to survive.

༼ "We have these fantastic arguments. Not often, even now . . . but when we slip into them, they accelerate . . . from nothing up to these crashing encounters, intense . . . pitting these fast, hard, icy raps against each other . . . like sound-tracks, scripts . . . late at night . . . ."

"You're stressed," Dr. George says. "Heather's sick, she's worn out. You're taking care of her, you're worn out."

Leaving the office I catch sight of a patient I knew from the ward, loitering on the street. Bony, bald, whisker-bleared; yet still with the glittering, seeking eyes. Shining from half a block away. He sees me and makes for me, hob-bling. I hurry the other way. These days I feel none of the kinship, warped nostalgia, I have often felt meeting such ghosts. *Non-fellowship was a first small step out of hell.* A les-son I learned while recovering on the suicide ward. Now I feel the same indifference to the outside world, the same non-sociability as I draw deeper, pulling any strength I can find in after me, inside the close nourishing circle of the life Heather and I have built together—"the delicate web," Heather has called it, not recently but in better days.

Inside the car, I check the cell phone. No messages. I feel my chest expand in relief. Heather and I would quite happily have gone through life without ever owning a cell phone, but at some point early on one of the doctors made our getting them a condition of not hospitalizing Heather immediately. I welcome its ring—only Heather has the num-ber, so I know she will be on the other end—but I never hear it without a start of alarm.

ଓ   On the other hand (thinking of the Hitler frogs again), such fancies are not just distractions. We have need of crazed ideas just now; they are the only ones with any chance of proving useful. Heather with her frogs: the comfort of the hybrid, the fecund, the transforming; the alien human, with distorted and exaggerated features, clownish, a crayon scrawl of the idea of hands, feet, legs, arms. Eyes, mouth. Face. At a certain depth of illness the mind is not helped by depictions of wholeness, which seem too far-fetched to be useful; what it can perhaps make use of and assimilate, and so gravitates toward, are images of fractured lucidity, evidence that even a shattered mirror can be pieced together, if never fully restored. Hitler and the cane toad, the poison dart frog; the lurid, brilliant colours; the ghastly toll to take Berlin: it is a way of simplifying our mental diet while also keeping it congruent with the radically altered, fantastic world we are occupying. Even if the irrational does nothing else, it attests and affirms that which is real but unexplainable.

When I saw—or finally registered—the change in Heather's eyes—now so wide and luminous; an unremittingly intense, yet somehow vacant, somehow absent stare—I knew beyond doubt that she had entered that zone where wonder and terror are the only law, two sides of the same diamond-chiselled commandment. She was living there now. And I knew that wariness, as much as love, would be required on my part. What was taking shape inside her would take the space it needed and, according to its own parasitical laws, drain whatever nutrients it required for its own development. It would not be overruled; it could only be subverted, its power drained or diverted, delicately and patiently.

Each night, after Heather has been ambushed into sleep and I have eased the book from under her hands, I look at the picture she was last looking at, trying to catch the same glimpse she was seeking, a fleeting likeness. She does not leaf through the book; she turns to one of a small number of pictures. From these, the several frogs she returns to repeatedly, I have a small gallery in my own mind of the images she is contemplating—as comfort, as sketches of elucidation, as, I believe, animal analogies of her own soul's state.

Besides the paradox frogs there are the glass frogs, of such seemingly absurd delicacy, with their thin, translucent skin that makes visible their beating heart and other internal organs; wood frogs, who permit themselves to be frozen solid all winter, knowing that, by the sugary antifreeze they manufacture in their veins, they can revive and breathe again in the spring; tree frogs, with sticky pads on their fingers to cling fast to steep surfaces and at perilous heights; the blackened, fossilized skeleton of a primitive frog, one from Pangea, the ur-continent, an anonymous participant in the exodus that took the frogs, one hop at a time, to every corner of the globe.

ɞ One day in July, I find myself wondering if I can give Heather a poem I have written. Normally this would not be a ticklish proposition; I have given her dozens of poems, after all—but these are ticklish times. It is not just that she is touchy and irritable, often volatile; nor is it just that the poem is about her (or, allusively, about me, us, *it*). It is also because I know (and sometimes I wish I didn't know so much about this business; I feel like a computer whose psychiatric database is so overloaded that it sometimes freezes at a simple input or command) how discerningly apocalyptic the disturbed eye is. It is drawn to reflections of itself, its own rigorous distortions, but it has a cold, even cruel, power of appraisal and won't accept amateur knock-offs. It

rejects with particular indignation paint-by-number productions, blandishments or pep talks that, by offering false
consolation, make all consolation false. Sick spirits are
most likely to be bolstered by enactments from the same
operatic stage they are living on, screams or swan songs
that forecast doom with brio, that is to say, that forecast
life.

Don't think—don't overthink . . . the counsel I most
commonly give myself these days. Above all, I am afraid of
Heather and I becoming too tortuous-tentative with each
other, of losing all our normal ease of being together. I don't
want to become so fearful of exposed wires that I can't turn a
light on.

But when I go down the hall to the studio, where she
has wandered in the hope of resurrecting one of the works
abandoned weeks ago, she is standing in the centre of the
room with her hands slack at her sides, her shoulders
slumped, looking away from the untouched painting out the
window, which shows only the dusty gravel on the rooftop of
the building next door. How can I poke my production, even
though it is only four lines long, into such a picture of cre-
ative desolation?

Later, when she has gone to work, I leave it on her
desk with a note penned at the bottom of the page: "a frog
poem for heather. with love from mike."

Midnight

*Through a long cold spring dark tadpoles battened on
    their tails
in roadside ditches, watching pin-eyed what came near.
Those pools stand dry. Starlit beings, emerald in fear,
tense to go springing into sunlight, grasses, pails.*

Entering the apartment later that evening, after my own shift has ended, I see that she has taped it up on the wall above her desk.

ೞ Camp, which I attended during my tenth and eleventh summers, occupies the place in my consciousness where no pleasure is guiltless. More than "fun," which I barely recollect, *camp* to me means fear, struggle, and shameful collusion. Even when I lived there, camp was less a physical place than a state of mind, a synonym for degenerate pastimes, acts of offhand violence facilitated by craven collegiality. It was a time of toxic cruelty, practised alone but more feverishly in packs of boys, which may have been mostly the result of accumulating sex hormones that had found as yet no other outlet. There was a sense of sickened, rapturous release, of throttled ugly powers violently vented, as when a boil is lanced, that came from the infliction of deliberate pain on smaller, weaker creatures. On occasion—usually near the end of a night of drinking, in tones of shamed amazement —other men have confided similar experiences of a time of secret and absorbing torment, a psychopathic interval that fell like a shadow between childhood and the start of seeing girls. (Heather, though she remembers her own brand of "twists" from childhood, has no memories of this kind; I don't know if many women do.)

Of my many tainted memories of camp, given what has been happening lately, it is the carnage we visited on the frogs that has been returning to me.

We used frogs as meat, as bait for meat, and as objects of pure torture. The bullfrog, *Rana catesbeiana*, was the one we hunted for frog's legs dinners. Slipping, in a canoe or poled skiff, up a sluggish stream, a jagged seam of tea-coloured water dividing shoals of overlapping lily pads dotted with white-and-yellow flowers, we sight the biggest bullfrogs hunkered down near the thick, high reeds where the mud starts. The counsellor at the back shows us how it is done. Like bulls in an arena, the bullfrogs are deceived and slaughtered with the help of a bit of red cloth. The square of cloth, ripped from an old shirt or sheet, is attached to a thick steel hook, which is attached in turn by a few feet of heavy string to a long pole made from a stout, peeled branch. Quietly, we lift our baited hook toward the "bullies" by the bank, lifting it as high as we can above the smaller, intervening bullfrogs, some of whom make vain jumps at it; they have moved out to more exposed positions on the lily pads for fear of the larger frogs, who, like them, will eat anything that moves and fits in their mouths. The square of red cloth must look to them like the feast of a huge, slow-moving insect. We bring it within range, perhaps with an animating flick or two—and crash! the bullie lunges and impales himself through his gaping mouth on the barbed hook. They gyrate and twist upwards with their long legs, at the same time pushing with stubby arms, to try to free themselves. We laugh at that. Grasping their back legs—which squirm thickly and with real kicking power, meaty as babies' legs—we swing them hard against the side of the boat (or against rocks when we hunt them from land), braining them repeatedly (their skulls are hard), then, when pink tongues and froth have billowed from their mouths, dropping them in our pail. Sometimes they scream—after the hooking, during the brief handling, or after an ineffectual attempt at braining. The scream, more a keening wail, is high-pitched and very human-sounding. It sounds like raw terror mixed with a hoarser note of outrage. There is something else, which I had forgotten until this moment. Sometimes, when their legs are pinned, we kiss them. Not as a re-enactment of a fairy tale moment, but just because the taut, moist green skin between the great eyes is so tempting. And when we clean them, slicing them in half at the waist and peeling off the leg skin with pliers, we are amazed by, sincerely admiring of this dark, incredibly thin tissue, like a pair of opaque cellophane tights, and amazed by and admiring of the long naked legs underneath, the calf and thigh muscles bulging yet perfectly proportioned, like a ballet dancer's. They are miniatures of the adult legs that we, stringy or pudgy boys, would kill to have.

What shames me about those hunts is not the killing itself but rather the pleasure I took in it. Or, to be more precise, the pleasure I took in the degradation and powerlessness that preceded it. I was squeamish actually about the splats and sprays of the braining, but I knew even then that such squeamishness is of little or even negative moral value. The bullfrog was snatched from mid-bullie-life in the sun, and killed without delay (apart from a perverse kiss) and, probably, fairly painlessly; could I say the same, would I scruple as much, about the animals whose remains fill the bags in my freezer? In retrospect what worries me more than a murder for meat is the tingling pleasure I felt, warm waves of it in the viscera and groin, at wielding absolute power over another living thing: trapping it, watching it writhe and contort itself helplessly, pinning (and kissing) it, hearing it wail in terror. It was a consummation; it lit up wicked pleasure centres right in the centre of me. It hit me, on the cusp of sexual maturity, not just where I lived but where I was going to live—in a carnival of sadism and masochism, random sparkings of violence directed outward and, increasingly, inward, a graph of oscillations and explosions that finally, in exhaustion, I agreed to label as madness.

But this has jumped too far into the bushes, and needs to return to the water and the frogs. As largemouth bass bait, nothing surpassed the little "greenies," thumbnail-sized, just-hatched (in early July) leopard frogs, *Rana pipiens*. A greenie cast at the edge of a line of lily pads brought the bass, waiting for just such a fortuitous splash, lunging out from underneath. I have described (in "Hunters in the Snow") how expert we became at catching the tiny frogs with both hands, filling a metal minnow bucket with forty of them in a one-hour stalk along the shore of a weedy bay. And there is no need to dwell on the snout-piercing hooks, the gymnastic escape attempts, the shrill screams or disconsolate groans—these were small-scale replicas of the bullfrog experiences. What I want to isolate is the further revelry in power, in the appetite for subjugation of the weak. A favourite pastime was to sit by the pail, listening to its muted croaks and chirps, the soft pings of leaps at its sides and lid, and then to quell these instantly by a Zeus-like rap of thunder with the knuckles on the lid. The tiny prisoners could be imagined so easily, cowering in the dark among rotting leaves and fetid water. When the hand went inside the parted lid to select a victim, there was the same sense, as fingers groped among wet small squirming bodies, of a hand from heaven, giant in command.

More focused and elaborate torture was the inevitable extension of these practices. BB guns, a new toy, facilitated it. With a weapon that could shoot across a small bay, or from the trees down at the waterline, there was no need even for stealth. The air gun's relative lack of power was a boon to a boy torturer; it didn't blast the target to smithereens, but made him jerk away in surprise and pain, a slower-moving target for more considered shots. And the lack of power meant that the copper balls often did not penetrate very far beneath the tough skin. You could see it shining in a leg muscle, like an incongruous ore vein surfacing. Once, a shot right between the eyes, that lodged but did not, apparently, even stun, made this frog seem to be sporting the fabled "precious jewel" or toadstone of amphibian lore, a round third eye of shining copper, ringed by an exciting ruby circle of blood. Torture gets elaborated, codified; as with pornography, its pleasures wane and must be escalated. Frogs are put in styrofoam containers with tops, introducing an element of randomness: Which of the blind shots will strike him, and where? Perhaps, in a version of Russian roulette, if he survives a certain number of shots unscathed (or not too scathed) he will be released; mercy, arbitrarily dispensed, is another prerogative of power. Floating on the river, sinking slowly as the shots aerate the box, he is a valiant captain in a doomed ship assailed by cannon fire, a figment of a boy's Trafalgar. Pulled, soggy and bleeding, from the wreck, he receives a respectful coup de grâce from his victorious adversary.

છ Why am I telling Heather this? I wonder, even as I am telling her. Telling her again—for, in our fifteen years together, she has heard all this before, in dribs and drabs. (One benefit of shared insomnia is that there is no shortage of time to talk; and when the hours stretch very late, during the pre-dawn blackness of 3:00 or 4:00 a.m., that is when the twists are likely to emerge.) Why now, why again? Am I telling her, from a sudden loss of faith, that I am unfit to help her, that I am too full of sick twists myself? Or could it be that I am telling her, reassuring her, that I *am* the right person to stand beside her through this? My support is not

159

lily-livered, automatic, unknowing, useless. I have been there, and come back. Come partly back, at least. Return is possible; the door swings both ways. And what more is being offered by these ruminations on the amphibian? Something of the best, crouching, burrowing, squirming, hopping, down in the muck of the worst? Hope in a larval state is here, of that I am sure, for Heather, strung out and reeling from her own chemicals and from the pharmaceuticals stirred into them, her focus scattered like dropped mercury, never listens more attentively or shares her own thoughts more eagerly, offering her unsentimental and clear-eyed (even now) perspectives on people and animals, dredging up through the drug bog arcane lore about amphibians that she has gleaned from her wide reading in anthropology and myth. The frog has become the image we are chasing, in sickness and in health. Chasing toward . . . ? Mercy, I think. Forgiveness—of something, or of many things. Of ourselves, perhaps, most of all.

Reconciliation? It is impossible to be precise about the quarry; the chase is on.

ᚉ   Boyish pranks, some might say of my camp days—or deviltry, as it used, more tellingly, to be called. But that would be naive. This violence, I sensed vaguely then and am sure of now, was the very root of violence—rooted and rooting. Even then I knew obscurely—an awareness signalled by the revulsion, a wallowing feeling, that was an admixture of my pleasure—that these sadistic revels were destructive of myself as well as of their more obvious victims. Further, that my future development as a person would hinge—for the acuteness of my absorption in torture meant that no negligible part of me was engaged in it—on how completely I could leave this violence behind. Not redirect it against myself—for that, I think, in some terribly complicated way, is what happened—but quit it altogether. It is a quitting (a "leavetaking," to borrow the last essay's term) that I believe I am making over a lifetime, and one, moreover, that I am making alongside—though I would hope at a faster rate than—society at large.

(And yet—something in me rebels at the portrait, over the last few pages, of my preadolescent self, which in highlighting his incipient bouts of blackness leaves out his still far more numerous sunny days and gentler pastimes. What of the photographs that show a lively, amiable, almost always cheerful boy? They were not a lie. Friends and family recall fondly the same good-natured boy; and even my own memories, scattered and ghostly as they are on that side of the break, attest him. I wonder if in focusing on these malignant streaks I am not behaving somewhat like Edward Gibbon, whose looming scenes of horror and waste—a good man's head on a lance, an empire auctioned by louts—deflect the reader from thoughts of the millions of Romans who might still have been living decent and honourable lives. My search is his in miniature: to try to pinpoint the moment (which in reality is unknowable) when marauders slipped past the gates in sufficient numbers to begin undoing the city. And it is perhaps easier, practically and emotionally, to picture fault lines of obvious fracture than to think of sanity dissolving by invisible degrees, slipping away imperceptibly, leaving no more traces than a few coins glinting out of rubble. And, too, there is a feeling—which I can't impute to Gibbon but must understand myself—of nagging pity, whose obverse might be hatred, for that boy of such promise who could not keep his mind from crumbling.)

Eastern cultures seem to have made better peace with the amphibian. So, apparently, had ancient cultures. A statue of the seated, smiling Buddha is not unlike a plump, placid toad or frog, basking by the lily pond. Early cultural records show amphibians naturally associated, not only with crop-sprouting rain, but with abundance generally, with fecundity, and with movement between the realms of life and death. In Chinese legend, Chang O stole the immortality elixir from her husband and fled to the moon; for this she was changed to a three-legged toad, but her husband, taking pity on her, built her a palace on the dark side of the moon; living on the sun himself, he can only visit her at the new moon when the sun shines on Chang O's palace. During the Moon Festival, celebrated at the full moon called the harvest moon in the West, moon cakes and moon-shaped fruits are offered to the toad that controls the dark (yin) half of Earth's year. Three-legged toads, carved from wood or stone, are symbols of prosperity. In folk religions that endure in India, elaborate marriage ceremonies are conducted for frogs in order to bring rain. (In 2003, as if to validate this practice, biologists found a never-documented species of purple frog, *Nasikabatrachus sahyadrensis*, in India's Ghats Mountains. It had eluded scientific notice for so long because it lives underground for fifty weeks of the year, emerging only to breed during the two-week deluge of the monsoons.) In Aztec Mesoamerica, the giant toad goddess Tlaltecuhtli, who controls the endless cycle of death and resurrection, was sometimes shown giving birth to the new world while swallowing the souls of the dead. Frog symbols on Sumerian cylinder seals, usually numbering nine, are thought to have been used to calculate a pregnant woman's due date. Cretan storage jars, from around 2000 BC, were decorated with frogs or toads under a sign thought to represent the womb. A millennium and a half later, in Aristophanes' *The Frogs*, Dionysus hears the frogs croaking "Brekekekex koax koax" as he is rowed across the river Styx. And in the ruins of Thebes, a frog-shaped terra cotta lamp was found, inscribed: *I am the resurrection.*

All of this frog symbolism came to magnificent fruition in ancient Egypt, a kingdom along the muddy banks of an annually flooded river, which would have been gifted (and sometimes cursed) with prodigiously prolific hatches every year. Heather's favourite Egyptian frog is the handsome little fellow, with green-and-brown marbled skin, perched pertly on a flat-topped stone or the lip of a small bowl, painted on the limestone stela of Prince Wep-em-nefret during the fourth dynasty reign of Khufu. In an early Egyptian creation myth (circa 3000 BC), four male frog-headed gods create, with their four female snake-headed consorts, the world; one of the eight, Amun, later becomes chief god; another, Heh, usually shown with a frog head, becomes the god of infinity and time, his upraised arms symbolizing 1,000,000, or eternity. Heqet, a later goddess of childbirth and fertility, is depicted with a frog's head and has a frog's character for her name. Heqet assists the birth of the sun god, Ra, from the underworld each night. Frog-shaped amulets to Heqet were made by the thousands, and knives decorated with frog's heads were laid on pregnant women to protect them. These amulets, which were first toad-shaped and then more frog-like, were thought to represent the human embryo and the developing fetus, in which case their use might have been equivalent to a prayer for the power to change safely.

Clearly, for ancient peoples around the world, it was natural to view frogs—with their loud croaking choruses (they are believed to be the first animal to have developed a voice), their breeding groups, egg masses and plentifully hopping offspring; with their quasi-human shape, four-limbed and great-eyed, hyperbolizing the leap and stare; and with their ability to change shape from egg to tadpole to adult and to move freely between water and land—it was inevitable to see them as agents of fertility and transformation, life, death and rebirth. And to honour them as such.

What happened? Why, by the late sixteenth century, is even Shakespeare unable to observe a common toad except through the fog of superstition in which it squats, "ugly and venomous" yet wearing "a precious jewel in its forehead?" (Though as usual with Shakespeare, there is no way of knowing whether he endorsed a ready-made view or just purveyed it shiningly.) But the Elizabethans are already very late in the long game of amphibian-bashing. It is hard to say when it began, but somewhere a wrong turn was taken, a deviation away from fluidity and bounty and into fixity and a cramped absolutism, which insisted on duality and pushed the traveller between realms deep into the interior, reviling him when he peeped out. One is tempted to wonder if the Israelites in Exodus, cursing Pharaoh with the plague of frogs (a plague of plenty which could result in heaps of decomposing froglets, as the captive Israelites probably witnessed: "And they gathered them together upon heaps: and the land stank." Exodus 8:14), were not calling back on their oppressors their own abundance, as we might say to a rich man oppressing us, "Keep your money—choke on it!" All of the curses—water to blood, frogs, locusts, murdered firstborn, even darkness, the yin-darkness of Nile mud—seem like perversions of a super-fecundity, vengeance on fecundity by an enslaved people desperate to flee back into a light-filled desert. Although Coptic Christians carved frogs in their catacombs, Christianity in the main condemned the amphibian. The Romans' frog-themed bronze weights, fountain bases and garden sculptures became heresy under the Christians, and John, in Revelation 16:13, sees "three unclean spirits like frogs come out of the mouth of the dragon, and out of the mouth of the beast, and out of the mouth of the false prophet." This demonizing of the amphibian, which still allows to fecund transformation an inverted potency, declines in Europe into pure superstition by the Middle Ages. In Boccaccio's *The Decameron* two lovers die after touching to their lips some sage from a patch that a toad has been sitting in (a fire is built to destroy the sage and the toad). In *A Thousand Notable Things*, a popular book from 1579 probably read by Shakespeare, Thomas Lupton tells how to obtain the mystical jewel hidden in the toad's forehead by putting the toad in an earthen pot in an anthill and letting the ants devour all but the toadstone. Toads were feared as witches' familiars or as ingredients used in their black masses, as in the cauldron scene in *Macbeth*. In Shakespeare's two dozen references to frogs and toads, not one of them is positive.

The catalogue of fancy becomes dreary; it scans like a dumbing-down, an embarrassment, a blind spot in the midst of a Renaissance. The "toady" was the mountebank's assistant who ate or pretended to eat a toad, the "poison" from which the master then expelled. The toad's supposed venom (the skin secretions of European toads are only mildly toxic), specially diluted and prepared by healers, was sold as charms and medicines at toad-fairs in England. Nostradamus spitefully called Frenchmen "crapauds," or toads, which in honour of the edible legs of *Rana esculenta* became the more durable "frogs" or "froggies." The fleur-de-lis, however, which began as "three toads erect, saltant," was changed to three lilies by the fifth century Frankish King Clovis, who, newly converted to Catholic Christianity and facing an army of Arians, is said to have seen in the heavens a new device of three lilies *or* on a banner *azure*—his *oriflamme*—which promised that the heretics would be successfully slain, and proved in that to be correct.

It is hard to avoid the conclusion that amphibians have been demoted in Western, now Christian-capitalist, culture because that culture is troubled by many of the things that amphibians represent. It is troubled by fecundity, unless that fecundity is sanctioned by the Church or its licensed affiliate, the Family. It is troubled by self-transformation, another kind of fecundity, unless the transformation is God-enabled and/or materially directed (televangelism and infomercials express, crudely, the accepted parameters). And it is troubled by shifting identity—again, related to transformation and so to fecundity—since identity is supposed to be fixed in the double sense of stable and repaired.

The development of rational science and the scientific method made frogs useful again, as readily available laboratory specimens with human-resembling anatomies, but it subjected them to procedures no less gruesome than the ones my cohorts and I devised as boys, albeit for (usually) more legitimate purposes. Leonardo da Vinci's dissection of a frog, in 1487, revealed that the brain controlled all other organs. A century and a half later, in 1628, William Harvey's dissertation on the circulation of the blood was based on frog dissections; not long after, Anton van Leeuwenhoek refined, by dissecting tadpoles, the model of the motion of the blood through capillaries. A green frog inside a black triangle, set in the floor of London's Faraday Museum, commemorates the research into the electrical basis of muscle contractions and other physiological operations pursued through frog dissections undertaken by Galvani and Volta, whose discoveries were pursued novelistically by Mary Shelley in *Frankenstein*. Frogs were central to the mid-twentieth-century research on DNA and cloning. From the 1940s onward, the African clawed frog, *Xenopus laevis*, was shipped round the world for use as a pregnancy test; if a pregnant woman's urine was injected into the frog, the frog would begin laying eggs. Even now, after the development of chemical tests, *Xenopus laevis*, which, with its pale colouring and small eyes with small or no eyelids set well back on its head, resembles human fetuses even more than most frogs, is the most widely used laboratory animal in the world.

A boy I tutor once told me, in a brash voice but with evasively flicking eyes, of how "horrible, but cool" it was to decorticate such a frog—kill it by running a wire repeatedly through its brain cavity—and then see its legs twitch by touching electrodes to the muscles.

"For what kind of experiment?" I asked.

"Between experiments," he said.

~ By August we are both exhausted, dragging ourselves through our days. This summer, we agreed early on, would have to be our summer of "being sick and just taking care of ourselves." Those minimal, unassailable imperatives were supposed to help us stay focused and save us from the stress of loftier ambitions. But being that and just doing that so doggedly have ground us down all the same. Between us, we take twenty-nine pills a day—mood stabilizers, antidepressants, anticonvulsants with (hoped for) antikindling properties, omega-3 fatty acids and vitamin supplements—handfuls of which we swallow at the kitchen sink at intervals throughout the day. Heather's lithium and escitalopram levels have not changed lately, but her lamotrigine dosage has been increased three times. She tolerates the side effects of these drugs better than I ever did—her queasiness, dizziness, grogginess and blurred vision increase with each rise in dosage but soon, over a few days, subside to "background" levels—but also, perhaps due to the same tolerance, the regulatory effects of the drugs plateau quickly. Her symptoms keep "breaking through": panic, depression, agitated confusion. One hopes for skill and knowledge from the doctors, but watching them lay on more pills, trying to damp this thing down, the image that comes to mind is of someone—I have done it many times myself—trying to secure a package that contains objects of irregular shapes and sharp edges, winding the plastic tape around it in fierce spirals, around and around, swathing and swathing until it is lumpily muffled, sometimes—paranoia and fatigue combining clumsily—passing the dispenser over the name and address accidentally. The promise and pursuit of health have left Heather feeling dazed, diminished, drained—*carrying, dragging . . . something heavy*—while, still, she is dangerously unwell. One night when I am sitting on the edge of the bed, keeping her company while she waits to fall asleep—insomnia is breaking through too, as the drugs' sedative properties wear off—she says, "I can't believe I'm here." It is a calm report. Her eyes don't have their lurid flares, nor their turbid eddies. They look tired. Blank apertures, with puffy dark circles around them. *Cancelled*, I think—the word pops up like a fright figure in a film, and I run mentally from it, even though it is a word I have used often about myself and have even made, at times, a kind of resigned peace with. (At a reading once, a listener asked, "How can you write so convincingly about the afterlife?" And the answer, which I would not say, popped into my head from Writing 101, the Irony Unit: "Write what you know.")

Not for Heather. Not this time, I think, fiercely and helplessly.

She suggests playing chess in the evening; maybe that will sharpen her concentration, force her to think through the haze. Reluctantly, I set up the pieces. Her game begins with her usual sharp attack but soon stumbles into blunders.

(Just as, twenty-seven years ago, when I was convalescing at home for the first time, my Scrabble game fizzled—my brothers and sisters wide-eyed with pleasure at beating me—beating their older brother, beating the writer—and then wide-eyed with fear when they realized that the win was no fluke, they could beat me anytime, easily; "cat" and "dog" and "box" were only intermittently available to me.) In the muddled midgame, Heather nods off at times; we chat desultorily, and invent our own version of stalemate when neither of us can remember whose move it is.

The *delicate web*—as Heather, in happier times, dubbed our insular home routines—has to be drawn smaller and closer, its strands simplified and tightened. We stay in mostly, except to go to work, and try to get at least the animal things right: stocking food, eating, sleeping. (Tidying up is sporadic and cleaning almost non-existent, we are simply too wiped, so the burrow grows progressively chaotic and grimy.) It feels sometimes as if we are painting ourselves into a corner, but it feels necessary. We say no to social invitations. We don't get many; back in June, persuaded or exhausted, Heather acceded to my arguments and told her family and a few close friends the basics of what was happening; they expressed concern and/or bewilderment and have since backed away, giving her space. We call or e-mail less often; siege reports, in their monotony, are difficult for both parties. After numerous discussions, Heather decides not to attend my mom's eightieth birthday party at French River. Recent "meltdowns," at work and at home, show that her state is too precarious for the complexities of a family gathering at a distance; better she stay home and try to harvest a few hours rest. But can I leave her alone, even for just one night? I try to imagine her by herself in the apartment, but it is difficult; the picture goes blank or gets frightening. She wants me to go, though, and promises that she will not do anything "bad" or "stupid." Looking into her eyes, I trust this; I want to and have to. What I see is an extremely tired person who wants mainly to sleep. Still, I drive off with my stomach knotted. You can extort a promise, but not the modicum of stable health it will take to honour it. Twenty-four hours later, after my family has seen my mother through her eightieth summer, as they saw me through my fiftieth a year ago, I am speeding back down Highway 400, arriving home by 11:00 p.m. Pressure in my chest unlocking the door, hearing nothing from the other side.

Heather is dozing on the couch. She is all right. Some bad moments, but . . . "I'm here."

Here.

ᘓ Our trip north to Temagami is begun with expectations so low they barely clear the event horizon. It is the only way we can begin it at all. We have the directions to a cabin on an island and a reservation for the night of Saturday, August 19. It is a six-hour drive; if we complete it, we will stay the night; depending on how that night goes, we may stay another. This can be extended for up to seven days, the week of our holidays.

Temagami means "deep water off the rocks," the owner tells us in the office as we check in. Already it is almost more information than we want. Her husband takes us to our cabin in a cedar grove and shows us, with pride, the TV with satellite hookup, running through a sequence of buttons to be pushed on the two remotes that I find hard to follow and only pretend to take in. "We don't even have a television in Toronto," I say, not meaning it to sound as numb as it does. He looks confused and a bit crestfallen.

Parts of the cabin are well-cleaned, but in the other parts there are a lot of spiders. Spiders and, of course, spider webs. Heather comes out of the bathroom and says, "There's a big wolf spider in there, up above the door." I go in and look up at him, flexing his legs. A few minutes later, as I am unpacking our small bag, she says, "Now he's got a friend with him." She is normally quite nonchalant about spiders and insects, but now her voice has an anxious edge; she is standing in the middle of the kitchen, well away from the walls, chewing a cuticle. I go into the bathroom and observe the two above the door, and while I am watching them, a third drops down on a line in front of the mirror. I find the vacuum cleaner and suck them up. Then go through the cabin clearing out all the webs and strands I can find. Run the narrow nozzle along beams, window ledges, corners, any-where I see white film or even sense it, anywhere particles are collecting suspiciously.

That night we eat the bread and cheeses we have brought, drink a bottle of wine, and go to bed early. Breathing clean air in the utter blackness of the cedar grove, we sleep nine hours, awaking refreshed and amazed. Neither of us can remember the last time we had a sleep that deep or long. Two or three hour catnaps are frequent with us; spotty four to six hour stretches the norm; the rare seven restor-ative, but also unrepeatable, the system shocked perhaps, so that the next night shreds back down to snatched naps. Nine? Waking with luxuriant slowness (for the insomniac, though sodden with fatigue, never sinks very far under and so starts flapping right away), we murmur with amazed de-light at our pleasurably weighted limbs, cleared and constant vision, patient nerves; and we murmur envy of the good sleepers, the ones who get this regularly: *This must be what it's like. Imagine.* Sips of the coffee hit the brain like lines of good cocaine. Sips of water do, too; our bottles of Life Brand taste glacier-fed.

Over in the office, I sign us up for a week and rent a canoe.

ɞ Dock-sitting agrees with us. We do a lot of it, more each day: listening to water lapping, watching sunsets; watching a smallmouth bass minnow, the caudal spot of orange and the black-fringed tail unmistakable, nip at particles we can't see on the surface. The water, limpid and green-tinged from the encircling spruce and cedar, is astonishingly clear; when I poke my paddle at a shoal just under the canoe, the water takes the length of it without my touching the rock. We take long paddles to nowhere in particular, or to non-urgent sites of interest: a high lookout ridge, an abandoned copper mine, a trail through old-growth pines. Often, on our small deck or on the dock, we are sitting so nearly motionless, talking little if at all, that animals approach us closely and without fear. A Gadwall duck. Paddling splashily, jump-flapping from one side of the dock to the other, then walking straight down it toward us. Flycatchers, hummingbirds, downy woodpeckers, various warblers. The usual chipmunk. They all come casually up to us. We are like carved seated statues of Bipolar Recovery, which nothing need fear approach. We eat simply and well, barbecuing meat and vegetables, drinking a bottle of wine each night. The eight or nine hour sleeps continue, miraculously, a run such as we have never had in our fifteen years together. They are almost eerie, in their depth and dreamlessness—as if we are two drained batteries plugged into an adapter of oblivion each night.

Once while we are sitting on the dock, Heather tells me that she is thinking of expanding the Persephone series of woodcuts she has just begun. So far she has key blocks for

"Leaving Winter's Mantle," the naked Persephone dropping her Queen of the Underworld robe and beginning the long climb up the root steps of the cavern toward where Demeter leans down, extending a hopeful hand; and "Undertow," already mentioned, which shows her sucked back down by the muscular tyrant, Hades. Now she thinks she might add two or three more images: Persephone in full summer mode, full winter, maybe the edgy-slumberous start of fall; round out the picture. Listening, discussing the possibilities, I try not to let a nurse-hovery tone invade our normal talk about art. Still, I can't help thinking, with a thrill of hope: *Four* seasons. Not *just* the rape into winter, or the slow drag-up to spring.

Another time, she asks if I've thought more about the thriller novel that we sketched out during our walk past the old copper mine, with its creepy abandoned trucks from the 1950s, garishly coloured and upholstered with shattered glass and pine needles, and on into the cool, moist, twilit spaces of the old-growth forests. An insane neo-Druidic cult, we imagined, persisting in human sacrifice and other bizarre rituals in the age of the Internet (and satellite TV)—we had fun turning it over, elaborating the characters and possibilities. I still like the idea, I say, but don't admit to Heather that I know I will never write it. Still, seven months after finishing the essays of *Leavetaking*, I can't imagine writing anything again. At first I put the extended blankness down to the depths of memory and trauma from which I'd had to pull that material up into words. The well had truly been drained this time. And then, more recently—as I still wrote nothing, felt no desire to write anything, apart from the occasional anxious "Midnight"—Dr. George started to call it "caregiver exhaustion." Worry night and day about Heather. Knowing a hundred things that might help, knowing nothing that definitely would. But caregiver exhaustion, like the drained well, still seemed inadequate to account for just how completely used-up, dried-up—*done*—I felt these days. Sometimes I suspect that the final irony of the enigmatic word *leavetaking* will be its literalness: I will remain engaged, for however long it takes, by the process of finishing up, of saying farewell, that my life has become. I think this often, but briefly, shying away from it to busy myself with chores or other distractions, as people do when their lives have become too painfully empty to consider. And this old, used-upness I feel runs so counter to the youthful ebullience that so many people have remarked on as a hallmark of my personality (that, indeed, finally corroborated for me the diagnosis of chemical disorder; as I said to one psychiatrist, "When I'm not in hell, I feel great."), that I wonder if there is not something Dorian Grayish about chronic mental illness, in that part of me is arrested in boyish, pre-illness exuberance, while the grimly coping part, the ill portrait, becomes wizened and shrunken. It is an over-simplification, an analogy only—but then so, in part, is illness itself.

It is after this particular dock talk, and the reflections that spiral from it, that I notice more cracks in the picture of our restorative week away that I, that both of us, have been so carefully daubing. Partly we are so surprisingly good at this relaxing, this drift, because neither of us can imagine resuming our life at home: where it might lead, what it might entail. Sometimes—often, now that I allow myself to see it—I catch Heather standing uncertainly in the middle of a room or on the dock, her eyes unfocused or flitting around at nothing in particular; sometimes chewing a cuticle or twining her hair. It wasn't just the spiders. Although a spider is a good image to crystallize fear, looped labyrinths of uncertainty with a fat dark dread lurking in the middle, the terminus of every anxious passageway. Such a spider soon appears.

At Heather's soft cry one morning, I come out to see her pointing at the rocks beside the dock. The spider (a nursery web spider, we will learn after we get home and visit the library) is very big and dark, with long, long legs. It has, as Heather says, "a weird, pushed-up sort of face," scrunched up skyward by the swollen whitish ball beneath it; not its distended abdomen, as we think at first, but a huge egg sac it is holding clamped in its chelicerae. When I scatter a bit of sand at it, it scuttles down into a crevice; but not too fast, and not too far; a few seconds later, the legs are peeping pugnaciously out again. After this first sighting, Heather never walks onto the dock without glancing over to ascertain the spider's whereabouts. I glance over too. Soon we have to glance both ways; the next morning, the same spider or its mate—it looks the same but there is no egg sac—is positioned on top of a quilty, funnel-shaped web, like a small white cornucopia, that it has woven around a bunch of slender spirea branches on the other side of the dock. Between its rock lair and this new construction, it seems to have laid a kind of claim to the dock, our dock, and we pass now through a sentry-guarded doorway to walk or sit on it.

The television, which we spurned at first, comes in handy after all. Scrolling through its channels, which number into the hundreds, is a good antidote when Heather becomes jittery and tired in the evening, a pattern from home that now resumes despite our lengthy sleeps. There is a lot of channel-scrolling to find a few interesting, and a couple of absorbing, programs. The most absorbing is a documentary on the wood frog's hibernation. Heather calls me from making dinner to watch it with her. We know, from our book at home, of the astonishing ability these northern frogs have to manufacture glycogen in their livers, turning their blood to a kind of sugary ooze that allows their bodies to freeze solid through the winter and then unfreeze safely in the spring. It is one thing to know this; it is another to watch it happen. A scientist in a white coat puts several wood frogs on a tray and places the tray in a freezer (this brings on an aversive sense of déjà vu, but despite his clinical procedures the scientist seems a true and kindly enthusiast about the frogs). There is a video camera in the freezer. As we watch, the frogs' breathing slows, and slows, then finally stops. Frost crystals cluster, coating them all over, including their eyes, which stay open. The scientist brings them out of the freezer, picks one up and flicks it (again that aversive prickle), then bobbles it in his hand: hard as rock. But in the tray left out on the table, the process has begun to reverse itself; in time-lapse photography, compressing several hours into minutes, we see the ice crystals melt and slide off; the skin soften in appearance, becoming less brittle and more rubbery-looking; one frog, the fastest thawer, draws a breath, a twitch in his small side; after long moments, another breath; then other frogs are breathing, small sides lifting and falling; finally, one makes a small hop. Alive.

Down to zero—close to it—and back again. Neither of us says a word. There is nothing to be said; we saw it.

On our last day, we take the last sections of our watermelon in a plastic bag and paddle to a quiet bay we visited before. Heather turns around in her seat to face me and we drift in the deep green shadows of the pines and cedars, eating pink watermelon and dropping the gnawed rinds into the bag. It is a moment of perfect restfulness, and it ends with a perfect, miraculous discovery. We have seen only one frog up here, a large leopard frog that hopped away once as we landed the canoe. The nights have been cold for late August, a few aspens already tinged with yellow. But today, when we stop on shore to stretch our legs, I see movement in the pine needles at my feet. I am a few moments spotting the small frog, his browns are blended so perfectly with the needles and rock and lichen. I put down my hand and trap him easily; he barely squirms inside my fingers. When I show him to Heather, parting my fingers to let his upper half pop out, then pinning him gently by the legs, we are amazed to see that it is the wood frog from the TV documentary. His black, robber-mask eye markings cinch it. It seems providential somehow, a sign, and standing on the rock admiring then releasing him—he hops away unhurriedly—we are both too moved to speak.

Heather, who has paddled in the bow all week, suggests that she try paddling us home herself. She stays facing me and begins moving us homeward, awkwardly at first, unsure of her steering, having to switch from side to side, but then strongly and more steadily, smiling with shy disbelief as her J-stroke returns to her. It is wonderful to watch; and hard in a way, too. Mental illness—meaning, here, the diagnosis and treatment of it, especially—is working against her confidence, implanting radical doubts in her about her basic capability. It is one of the reasons I feel so strongly that hospitalization should be avoided except as a last resort. If diagnosis means that one is being considered seriously for a position, then hospitalization is confirmation that one has got the job. And it can be a hard position to leave; it can easily become a career leading to retirement, and beyond.

CR   On the drive home from Temagami, I see an image of true horror. By "see" I mean that I know I am not dreaming it, and I know that I am not seeing it in the actual world (though it is hard to remain conscious of that fact). It is like a semi-transparent slide positioned between me and the world, which by an effort I can look through, deliberately unfocus, to concentrate on what I am supposed to be seeing, but which looms up, clear and vivid and right in front of me, whenever my concentration wavers. It is more like a waking dream than a hallucination, though neither term is very precise. I can only guess at its origins, too; from its detailed vividness, it seems like something I have seen, perhaps many times, or dreamed intensely, but I suspect that it is a collage of recent sights that my unconscious mind is presenting as one vision. Actually, the detail and vividness are what signal it is a construction: I can "read" it in any direction, up or down, side to side, without any blurring or discontinuity, like a gleaming reproduction in an art book. Life's glances, even life's close scrutinies, don't allow that; only our picture-making, storytelling faculties do.

At any rate, it is several hours, almost the whole of our drive, before the image begins to dissolve in places and fade, just pieces of it continuing to assert themselves, like bits of a more fragmentary and vile Cheshire cat.

What I see for those hours is the wood frog trying to swallow the nursery web spider. (An attempt I know is possible; amphibians are ravenous, indiscriminate carnivores; one study counted 1000 "items" disappearing into a toad's mouth in the course of a day.) The frog has its mouth clamped tight, but two long, strong-looking brown legs, protruding from the sides like waxed moustache ends, are clamped with equal determination to the sides of his jaw. This locked contest—neither party moves while I watch—seems enigmatic as well as horrible. The enigma is a part of the horror. It seems as if the frog should be able to overpower the spider and gulp it down, as it has already halfway done, but perhaps the spider found a chance, in the moment of its seizure, to inject some venom, and the frog is partly paralyzed, or its mouth is. Which creature will prevail? The amphibian, which in arachnid terms has only recently crawled up on land, or the web spinner? The frog has especially powerful stomach acids, as indiscriminate gobblers must; but the spider has to reach them first. What I see is a perfectly frozen tableau of attack and defense in all its raw, straining undecidedness. Each time I see it again, nothing has shifted; it still looks to be an equal contest.

Six days after our return, the downswing presaged by the frog-spider image occurs—but it is mine, not Heather's. It takes me by surprise; apart from stress and worry—and Dr. George's caregiver exhaustion—I have felt stable and sane these last few months, so much so that I grew sure that only Heather was in need of careful monitoring. After a few days of mild depression, I awake from an only averagely bad sleep, spend an unremarkable morning, and then, by noon, am hurtling straight down. The onset is so sudden that I have a whooshing sensation of freefall, and familiar internal feelings of a rapidly dispersing poison, with hints of alkali metal in my mouth and sinuses. I am shivering in my chair, dropping things I try to handle, and lurching when I walk down the hall, as if the besieged brain cannot send coherent messages to my limbs. This is a classic plunge, such as I have not experienced in a year—as if I have been pitched off a cliff, or hauled down by Heather's deathly muscleman. At the start there is still enough lucidity for consecutive thought, all of it bad: self-loathing, humiliation and disgust, persecution, paranoia, the escape of suicide. But these, like the last familiar faces picked out by a terrified kid on a roller coaster, splinter apart as the ride speeds up; what is left is a frenzied carnival of pure sickness, shredded sights, scissored by violence. In terms of the experience itself, nothing has changed since I was seventeen or perhaps even younger. But in terms of my reactions to it, my handling of it, there have been

incremental shifts that, added together, make a huge difference. This is what I threw all that alcohol at in darkened
rooms. Worse. This is what I tried to out-duel with weed,
hash, acid, speed, coke, shrooms, peyote—hoping one fire
would douse another, or craziness overload and short-circuit.
Much, much worse.

Now I have schooled myself to do as little as possible . . . and wait.

Limiting input is essential. Give the glutton less to
feed on. Social encounters, especially, are out; human beings, with their complex intercutting agendas, offer the
maximum input in any situation. I phone Heather at work
to tell her I'll have to miss the meeting at our apartment to-
night, a gathering of artists that Heather, nudging back into
art, hopes to mount a show with. My role in the evening was
going to be marginal anyway, bartender and cheerleader
mainly, but from any vantage point now it is inevitable that
I will get toxically drunk and end up raving, to myself probably until the guests leave, and then to Heather until dawn. I
feel guilty that I can't support the venture, just when
Heather is starting to get her art legs back, but I know that it
is the right decision, the only decision possible today.
Heather doesn't question it; my voice is so halting and faint,
it must sound like an amnesiac speaking down a string-and-
tin-can telephone.

I lie on my side on the bed with the curtains drawn,
taking deep breaths. An old approach and still one of the
best. A half hour before Heather and her friends arrive, I
walk to a nearby park and begin slowly circling the quarter-
mile running track, walking along the grassy verge to lessen
the impact on my just-about-shot knees. Slow, mindless ac-
tivity; slow, deep breaths. When the joint pains become too
piercing, I sit on a park bench, eyes unfocused, concentrat-

ing on the slow cycles of respiration that gradually quilt the mind and quiet it. Something cries in a high, sharp voice from the bushes; curious, I walk toward the sound and see a whitish flapping near the streetlight. Later, my shoes soaked with dew, I am walking up and down streets of sleeping houses, passing a number of raccoons criss-crossing the streets to pick at garbage bags. Their fat amblings, truculent stares back at me, seem mildly comic and vaguely obscene; they troll for scraps like night janitors in restaurants, annoyed to meet a patron after close-up. The image tells me I'm back. Not all the way but near enough. I dig the cell phone out of my pocket. The display says it is nearly 4:00 a.m. Heather answers on the first ring, though she sounds sleepy. "Everyone's gone," she says. "Come home."

As I approach our closed door, with the same anxious flurries in my stomach I have felt on every approach the last few months, something occurs to me: The calmness and clear-headedness, the stability that, with a few exceptions, has held you up all through Heather's illness—was that *more* sanity than you're really capable of? Inflated sanity, inviting an inevitable correction? The question, which still trails clouds of the day's confusion, focuses more precisely as I turn the key: Could this meltdown be a sign of faith in Heather's returning health? *She can handle this now,* I must have known on some level.

As if in answer, she is waiting just inside the door. As we embrace, she pats my back, murmuring, "This is the way it's going to be. You, then me, then you . . . . The way it's always been. First one, then the other. Me, you, me . . . ." She repeats it slowly, in different versions, so that neither of us can mistake it.

CR   "Caregiving *is* exhausting," Dr. George says at our next meeting after my meltdown. "People lose it; there's a reason they use that phrase. They *lose it.* Suddenly, dramatically. It flies apart."

It seems like part of a conversation we keep returning to lately, about how to disentangle outside causes from inner ones. Having resisted so long, and then finally admitted, the concept of endogenous causes for my swings, I am finding it difficult now to return to a middle position where the causes come sometimes from outside, from life events. Causes sometimes endogenous, sometimes exogenous. To live between these possibilities, trying to judge which pertains most in a given situation, is the goal Dr. George seems to be trying to steer me toward, and the major focus of our recent meetings. Even seeming tangents are a part of it.

"You're talking me into having a future, aren't you?" I say, half joking, during one hour in Hamilton.

"I'm part of the conversation. Mostly you're talking yourself into it."

And on another day I remember, before Heather was diagnosed, before we had even registered how she was sliding; I have been spinning my "Why won't it finish?" about *Leavetaking*, a query repeated so often that it has become boring, the tic of a mild neurosis, which leads to a question that sounds casual, though it tightens my chest to ask it:

"I've been wondering lately when you cut me loose."

Dr. George smiles at that. "I don't cut you loose. You cut yourself loose."

"When?"

"When you're ready."

I think about that, staring at the wooden table. "That could be a while, I think."

Dr. George raises her hands, palms upward—a *Whatever*, or *So be it*, gesture.

ভ In 1988, in early July, I was sitting on the sidewalk outside the small airport building in Sioux Lookout, conscious that I was at a low point in my life. Not a point of madness or of poverty, this time—at least, not poverty of the material kind. Working for Indian Affairs, I had made thirty thousand dollars over the previous year, teaching Grades 3 to 8 on a fly-in reserve five hundred miles north of Thunder Bay. Most of the money had gone to pay down student loans; still, I had a couple of thousand left in the bank and was more flush than at any previous point in my working life; in sixteen years, my highest previous wage had been $4.60 an hour. But I had other reasons to be down. Life on the reserve had been dispiriting; exhilarating at times, but overall, depressing. Living on a strip of marshy land by a lake frozen for eight months of the year; transmitting The Man's curriculum to a community that often seemed devoid of purpose except as a holding tank for 250 souls who shuttled between two churches, the Hudson's Bay store and the airport, on a single dirt road that curved like a fish hook; surrounded by depressed and/or alcoholic people and their bewildered, anxious, frequently abused children. My relationship with the woman I had been living with for seven years was ending; within a month, we would see each other for the last time. Not because of the reserve or the year spent mostly apart, she said; just because. Writing poems, the centre of my life eight years before, had dribbled to a halt. I was turning 33 in a month.

My main achievement, I felt, sitting on the curb surrounded by marsh and bush that, I knew from flying over it, stretched unchangeably for hundreds of miles in all directions, was staying out of hospital. In the late spring of 1979, I had been discharged; so far, I had not been readmitted. With a huge bag of tricks and tactics, with a warehouse of gambits and tools—with sheer bloody-minded will and hanging on—I had gotten by.

Apocalypse had been delayed, diverted, deferred. Had life, too? The question seems central to me now. I don't think the man on the curb considered it. He was too busy getting by.

Another difference between us is that I know, as he could not, that the dead end he thought he was staring at was in fact a crossroads. Up ahead lay apocalypse, but also life. In the next two years I would take up writing again, beginning modestly enough with a self-published book of poems, a selection from the two thousand or so I had churned out in my early twenties. There would be a resumption, too, of madness, announcing itself with a psychotic break that brought to a fiery end my three-year teaching career and launched—though that is the absurdly wrong word—me on a five-year career of psychiatric disability, on a low, then vanishing, then non-existent income. After nine simmering years—years of black smoking depressions and spurts of manic flame, both damped down by steady rains of alcohol—the mountain was about to blow up again, showering ash and molten rock, the ground shaking and fissuring apart, and the true glowing lava flowing down everywhere, burning or burying all in its path.

In that cataclysm, during it, I met Heather. It is impossible to summarize what she has meant to my life—but I think that in moving toward her, despite many seemingly impassable barriers, I was moving (unconsciously, instinctively, as a man parched with thirst moves toward the smell of water) toward someone who could lead me away from the

cruelty that had somehow, long ago, taken root in and disfig-
ured my life. Cruelty bent outward, first; and then, more ada-
mantly and severely, inward upon myself. Cruelty as a
blackly swirling maelstrom of forces, never tameable and
only rarely, usually to a deluded degree, even channelable.
Cruelty as imagination; cruelty as life. (Or: a cruelty that
permeated life and often got mistaken for it, a necessary part
becoming a tormenting whole.)

It was the past. It would be, in part, the future.

But not the whole part; not as big a part. Not with
Heather. As a person sick with cruelty borne and inflicted, I
could not but be drawn to someone so plainly and gracefully
adept at the art of mercy, or the mercy of art, a discipline ample enough to admit cruelty, even revel in it, without being
overwhelmed by it, without letting it hijack and terrorize the
whole story.

Something remarkable occurred that day in Sioux
Lookout, while I was sitting on the curb, waiting for the
plane which was always late. "The Miraculous Hatch" was
the natural title of the poem I later wrote describing the
event. But magical as it was, I could not see it then, sunk as I
was in the blind mire of depression, for the portent that it
seems to me now, from this vantage point eighteen years
later.

The only other person sitting outside that day was
an old man from Kasabonika, another reserve in the dis-
trict. He had leathery, very dark brown skin. We had exchanged a few words—establishing the basics of our places
and roles, as people in isolated settlements are especially
quick to do—when suddenly, tiny green frogs were hopping in every direction. There was no warning; no frog or
two, then three, hopping in advance. As if spontaneously
generated from the air, as used to be believed about many

living organisms, the small new leopard frogs, thousands of them, were simply there, here, everywhere, leaping and veering on what, moments before, had been bare concrete and tarmac. They hopped against us, feeling soft but vigorous, like ping pong balls batted with verve. They hopped against the walls of the airport building, fell down and hopped again, either at the same wall or in another direction. They hopped at the glass of the windows, against which other passengers were now clustered, gaping at the scene. The Kasabonika man, with a toothless smile at me, held up his hand; they jumped against it, over it, under it. I held up my hand; frogs hit it. When I held my palm level, some frogs landed in it, like splats of heavy green rain, then jumped off blindly again. A car dropping someone off crushed dozens of them, even at a slow roll; it slithered off, the wheels sliding on amphibian ooze, the driver half-blinded by green hail on the windshield.

I went inside. Only the Kasabonika man remained outside, though now he was staring off above the tallest reeds, above where the miraculous hatch had come springing from. His posture, relaxed and playful at the first taps, looked stiffly stoical now. The profusion got to you after a time, especially if your nerves were at all stretched thin. The sheer blind abundance, the veering plenty. And the insistence of the taps, like meek but dogged pokes; like dripping taps; like knocks on walls, on doors. No one else went outside.

It was easier to contemplate the marvel from behind glass. People were talking and pointing excitedly, laughing (gleefully but with a giddy edge); someone pointed at an approaching bank of huge black cumulus clouds, a billowing front sailing into this sunny afternoon, and then everyone started speculating about whether the approaching rain, some sense of it, had stirred the froglets to their odyssey. But to what purpose exactly? None of us knew.

Watching all of the frenzied motion, within the airport now as well as outside it, I experienced a moment of perhaps compensatory stillness. Whatever the cause, I was grateful in those days for any peace that was not mere leadenness. I was aware, too, of a sense of paradox, of unsustainable absurdity, that in its early phase was not unpleasant. The frogs were rushing frantically in all directions, even though it was not necessary to move at all, for soon, as the approaching storm made clear, the water would be everywhere.

ᘔ Midnight. I am drinking red wine on the futon in the studio, relaxing after work, watching Heather draw. She works more black into the base of the reeds above Ophelia. (We are still calling the large drawing "Ophelia," even though it departs in several ways from the scene Gertrude relays to Laertes. It is not daytime. There is no willow tree. There are no flowers.) Using the short stick of graphite, Heather works more black in, then takes some back again, eases in highlights, with presses of the gummed eraser that by now is itself black. The three lily pads in the lower right have gone too gray, especially the flower above one of them. She uses a knife to scrape some fibre layers from the thick paper, bringing the lily back up to white, a luminosity to match the drowned girl's upturned face. This oval of placid, cancelled beauty floats above the muddle of faster-sinking limbs and the fabrics swathing them, one half-submerged arm reaching out toward the lily pad and its bloom, in a way feebly counter to the slight but unmistakable bias of the head, tilted, as if hearkening to bad counsel, toward the black poisoned water under

187

the reeds, which, I agree with Heather, cannot be made too black.

We discuss some title ideas. (I envy Heather her ability to talk while drawing or painting, not needing to sever contact to create.) "Unto That Element," a phrase I recall from the passage in *Hamlet*, might work. Or something more simply descriptive, something tonal: "Reeds," "By Moonlight." Heather is patient about titles; they come to her in a flash, or not at all. Her fingers are black now, too; smears of it also on her jeans and shirt. Around the walls I see, tacked up, more new prints and sketches. They look like abundance, like life. Could it be over? This episode at least? I slap away the thought as tempting fate. Accept this night, this hour. It is surely enough.

After one of these hopeful, hoped-for nights, I turn back to writing, turn back to this.

Acknowledgements

I am grateful to the Canada Council for a grant which afforded me time to work on this project. And to the editors of *The Gettysburg Review* and *The New Quarterly*, in whose pages, sometimes in slightly different form, portions of this book first appeared.

I am fortunate to have as my publisher Dan Wells, who brings to his arduous trade energy, insight, tact, and unstinting regard for writing and writers.

Four friends read the first, shorter version of this manuscript and gave much-valued encouragement. Thanks to Dawn Pearcey, John Metcalf, Robyn Sarah, Sharon English.

I am most indebted to the two people who accompanied me on every step of the writing of this account and, even more critically perhaps, of the living with it afterwards: Heather Simcoe and Dr. Lindsey George.

A last, special thank you to Heather, not only for her unwavering support, but for her bravery, trust and generosity in allowing me to tell that part of this story which is hers.

About the Author

Mike Barnes in the author of six previous books: the novels *Catalogue Raisonné* and *The Syllabus*, the short-fiction collections *Aquarium* – winner of the 1999 Danuta Gleed Award – and *Contrary Angel*, and the poetry collections *Calm Jazz Sea* and *A Thaw Foretold*. Born in Minnesota, a joint U.S.- Canadian citizen, Mike lives and writes in Toronto.